Guide of Rome

THE ETERNAL CITY

IN NINE ITINERARIES

• Rome Map (back-cover)

• Updated useful information (page 114)

• Updated map of the underground (page 119)

LOZZI Roma

Rome is situated 41° 53' 54" N. lat., 12° 59' 53" E. long., on the banks of the Tiber. According to Varro's calculations, Rome was founded on April 21, 753 B.C. Rome was first governed by Kings (753-510 B.C.); then as a Republic by Consuls (510-30) and finally by Emperors (30 B.C. to 476 A.D.).During the Middle Ages, the Church established its temporal rule and Rome remained the seat of the Papal Court until September 20, 1870 when the Italian army entered Rome and the Eternal City became the capital of a united Italy.

The Vatican, a small territory of 0,440 kms.² occupied by St. Peter's Basilica, St. Peter's Square and the Vatican palaces, is under the sovreignty of the Pope, and it has been called the "Vatican City State" since 1929.

Rome has a population of over three millions.

The Kings of Rome. According to the legend, the seven Kings of Rome were: Romulus, Numa Pompilius, Tullus Hostilius, Ancus Martius, Tarquinius Priscus, Servius Tullius and Tarquinius Superbus.

667. Romans and Albans contesting for superiority agreed to choose three champions on each side to decide the question. The three Horatii, Roman knights, overcame the three Curiatii, Alban knights, and unite Alba to Rome.

509. Tarquin the Proud and his family expelled for tyranny and licentiousness: royalty abolished. The Patricians established an aristocratic commonwealth.

The Republic. First period (510-87 B.C.) from the expulsion of Tarquin to the Dictatorship of Sulla.

Second period (87-30 B.C.) from Sulla to Augustus.

496. The Latins and the Tarquins declared war against the Republic and were defeated at Lake Regillus.

477-396. Wars with Veii and the Etruscans. Veii taken by Camillus after ten years' siege.

390. The Gauls, under Brennus, won a remarkable victory over the Romans on the banks of the little River Allia, after which the sacked and plundered Rome. However, they eventually returned to their own land and Rome was gradually rebuilt (343-290).

264-146. The Punic wars, which culminated in the destruction of Carthage, the leading naval power in the Mediterranean.

146. The conquest of Greece.

88-86. Fighting between Marius and Sulla.

82-89. Sulla's dictatorship. Decline of the Republican institutions.

60-53. The First Triumvirate: Caesar, Pompey and Crassus.

58. Caesar's campaigns in Gaul and Britain.

48. Pompey was defeated at Pharsalus; Caesar was assassinated on March 15, 44 (the Ides of March), during a Senate Meeting.

43. The Second Triumvirate: Octavian, (the future Augustus), Anthony and Lepidus.

42. Battle of Philippi in Macedonia. Death of Brutus and Cassius.

31. Octavian defeated Anthony and Cleopatra at Actium (Greece); remaining the sole ruler of Rome.

The Empire. The Emperor Octavian (27 B.C.-14 A.D.) took the name of "Caesar Augustus". The birth of Jesus Christ. The reign of Augustus coincided with the golden age of Latin literature: this was the era of writers such as Cicero, Virgil, Horace, Ovid, Livy and Tacitus.

61. St. Paul visited Rome for the first time, entering the city by the ancient Capena gate. During Nero's reign and the Christians were blamed for the great fire.

70. Jerusalem was rased to the ground by Titus. Vespasian began to build the Colosseum in 72.

98-117. Under Trajan, the Roman Empire reached its maximum expansion.

117-138. During Hadrian's reign, Rome was at the peak of its architectural splendour. The Empire began to decline between the 2nd and 3rd centuries, as a result of internal crises and because of pressure from barbarian peoples.

272. Aurelius began to build the Aurelian Walls as protection against the threat of invasion.

284. Diocletian and Maximian: the first division of the Empire.

313. Constantine the Great allowed the Christians freedom of religious practice. In 331 he transferred the capital of the Empire to Byzantium (Constantitople).

395. The Roman Empire was definitively divided between the East (Arcadius) and the West (Honorius).

404. Transfer of the Capital to Ravenna.

410. Rome sacked by the Goths.

475. Romulus Augustulus, the last Emperor.

476. Odoacer's conqueror of Rome put an end to the Roman Empire in the West.

The Middle Ages. 493. The Goths established their reign in Italy, defeating Odoacer.

535-553. The Byzantine-Gothic war.

568. The Lombards invaded Italy. It was divided among the barbarians and the Eastern Empire (the Byzantines).

729. With the donation of Sutri by the Lombard king Liutprandus, the temporal rule of the popes began.

800. On Christmas day, Leo III crowned Charlemagne Emperor of the Holy Roman Empire.

1073-1085. Pope Gregory VII, a fervent and energetic reformer, began his fight against the Emperor Henry IV.

1084. Rome was invaded and sacked by the Romans, led by Robert the Guiscard.

1300. Boniface VIII proclaimed the first Jubilee.

1305. Clement V moved the papal seat from Rome to Avignon, where it remained until 1377.

1377. Cola di Rienzo, the last of the Tribunes, founded the Roman Republic. He was assasinated in 1354.

The Renaissance. 1471. The foundation of the Capitoline Museum, the oldest public collection in the world.

1503-1513. Julius II began to pull down the old St. Peter's in order to build the present Basilica, under Bramante's supervision.

1513-1521. Leo X, the son of Lorenzo the Magnificent, made Rome the greatest cultural centre. - Under the pontificate of Leo X the Lutheran Reform began. - The imperial invasion of Italy and the disastrous Sack of Rome (16 May, 1527) put an end to the golden age of the papal city in a nightmare of fire and blood.

1585-1590. Sixtus V, a real innovator of town planning, covered Rome with new buildings.

The Modern and Contemporary Age. 1799. The Jacobine Republic in Rome, pope Pius VI was deported to France.

1800. The First Restoration: Pius VII was re-established in Rome.

1809. Rome came once more under french hegemony.

1814. The Restoration brought back Pius VII to Roman soil.

1861. On March 27, the Italian Parliament declared Rome the natural and indispensable capital of the new State.

1870. On September 20, Italian troops entered Rome through the breach in Porta Pia.

1929. On February 11, the "Roman Question" between the Church and the State was finally resolved by the Lateran Treaty, which came to be part of the Constitution of the Italian Republic.

1946. In Italy, the Republic was proclaimed in accordance with the June 2 referendum.

1962-65. The Ecumenical Council, Vatican II, was summoned by John XXIII and concluded by Paul VI.

1978. After the death of Paul VI and the pontificate of John Paul I which lasted one month, John Paul II the Polish Pope, acceded to the pontifical throne. He is the first non-italian Pope for more then four and a half centuries.

2000. Great celebration of the Holy Year.

2005. The death of John Paul II brought over three million faithful to Rome. On April 19, the German Joseph Ratzinger was elected Pope with the name Benedict XVI.

The Capitoline Hill • The Imperial Fora
The Colosseum • The Roman Forum and Palatine Hill

Once sacred to the Romans and the destination of the triumphal processions of victorious generals, the **Capitoline Hill** is today the headquarters of the mayor and municipality of Rome. In spite of changing events and historic conditions, it has remained at the very center Roman life. It is reached by the great flight of steps known as the "Cordonata," built according to designs by Michelanglo for the triumphal entry of the Emperor Charles V in 1536. At the top of the stairs are the colossal **Dioscuri**, two sculpture groups from the late Imperial period, which were found near the Jewish Ghetto and placed here in 1583 by Pope Gregory XIII. **Piazza del Campidoglio** was designed by Michelange-

lo for the magnificent Pope Paul III (1534-1549). The old artist placed on a new pedestal the equestrian statue of the Emperor **Marcus Aurelius** (161-180), the only surviving example of the many bronze equestrian statues which once adorned Rome. It is commonly believed that this statue owes its preservation to the fact that it had been mistaken for a statue of Constantine, the first Christian Emperor. Michelangelo had the statue brought from the house of Verus - a descendant of Marcus Aurelius - in 1538. A copy was placed out on the piazza; the original statue, after long and delicate restoration work, is now kept in the large glass room in the Capitoline Museum.

The Colosseum.

Piazza del Campidoglio. The equestrian statue of the Emperor Marcus Aurelius (161-180).
Right, aerial view of the Campidoglio.

The Spinario.

Michelangelo also designed the two palaces on the opposite sides of the square, which are skewed to created a widening perspective effect.

Palazzo Senatorio, at the back of the square, was built in the 13ᵗʰ century on the ancient ruins of the **Tabularium**, one of the few surviving Republican era buildings. Constructed by Consul Quintius Lutatius Catulus in 78 B.C., it was the state archive of Rome, and bronze slabs with written laws and proclamations are still housed here. The facade of Palazzo Senatorio was designed by Giacomo dela Porta, and constructed by Girolamo Rainaldi. Michelangelo designed the double staircase and the fountain adorned by three statues: the *Tiber* and the *Nile* on either side, and in the center the Triumphant Rome. Above Palazzo Senatorio rises the **Torre Capitolina** (Capitoline Tower), erected by Martino Longhi in 1579. Descending to the right of Palazzo Senatorio, a small loggia to the side of the Tabularium offers an unforgettable view of the Forum, the most famous place in classical Rome, once rich with gorgeous temples, triumphal arches and monuments of all kind. To the right of the Roman Forum stands the Palatine Hill. The Palazzo Nuovo was built for Pope Innocent X in 1655 by Girolamo and Carlo Rainaldi; Palazzo dei Conservatori closes the

The Dying Gaul.

right side of Piazza del Campidoglio. The vast complex of the **CAPITOLINE MUSEUMS** is divided into multiple buildings which house some of the most important works of art in the world: Palazzo dei Conservatori, with the Conservator's Apartment (Appartamento dei Conservatori) on the first floor and the Capitoline Art Gallery (Pinacoteca Capitolina) on the second; **Palazzo Clementino Caffarelli** with the Capitoline Coin Cabinet (Medagliere Capitolino); Palazzo Nuovo and the Galleria Lapidaria: an underground tunnel that connects the Capitoline buildings and the **Tabularium**, on the ruins of which stand the Palazzo Senatorio.

Access to the Capitoline Museums is from **Palazzo dei Conservatori**: the palace erected in the mid-15th century over an existing structure, the building owes its name to the magistrates elected in ancient times. Below the monumental facade, a large portico opens onto the piazza. The central entrance leads to a courtyard, around which are fragments of a 12 meter tall statue of the Emperor Constantine, which once stood in the Basilica of Maxentius. The courtyard gives access to the staircase that leads upstairs. The building is home to many pieces of Roman sculpture:

among these is the original bronze **equestrian statue of the emperor Marcus Aurelius** (II century A.C.) in the Exedra of Marcus Aurelius, the large glass hall built by the architect Aymonino. The room, fulcrum between the older and newer parts of the building, stands on what used to be an open area (the so-called Roman Garden).

On the first floor there is the **Appartamento dei Conservatori**, official seat of Rome's city government, and the "Sala degli Orazi e Curazi" which was painted by Cavalier d'Arpino; the baroque painter Cesari worked here on and off for forty years. In the "Sala dei Trionfi" is the beautiful bronze statue of the **Cavaspina** (Boy pulling a Thorn from His Foot) or "Spinario". The statue portrays a natural, effortless attitude, and is the synthesis of a 5th

The She-Wolf.

View of Piazza del Campidoglio, with the Palazzo Senatorio in the background.

century B.C. head and a typically Hellenistic body from the 2nd century B.C. In the room of the She-Wolf, the **She-Wolf**, an Etruscan work of the 5th century B.C. which symbolizes Rome. In the 15th century, during the first flowering of the Renaissance, the Tuscan sculptor Pollaiolo added the figures of the two babies, which represent the twins Romulus and Remus.

On the second floor the CAPITO-LINE PICTURE GALLERY contains, among several important masterpieces of the 16th and 17th centuries: **Romulus and Remus** by Rubens; **Anthony and Cleopatra** by Guercino; **The Kidnapping of Europa** by Paolo Veronese; **St. Sebastian** by Guido Reni; **St. Petronilla** by Guercino; **the Magdalene** by Tintoretto; **the Gypsy Fortune-teller** and **St. John the Baptist** by Caravaggio; and portraits by Van Dyck.

Opposite the Palazzo dei Conservatori is the **Palazzo Nuovo**, which can be reached via the **Galleria Lapidaria** (opened to the public in 2005), an underground tunnel built in the Nineteen Thirties, eight meters beneath Capitol Square (Piazza del Campidoglio), to join the two buildings.

In the courtyard of Palazzo Nuovo sits the famous statue of **Marforio**, one of the so-called "talking statues" of Rome. A broad stairway leads to the first floor. In the "Room of the Colombe" is the **Mosaic of the Doves**, a work so fine that it might easily be taken for a painting. Found at Hadrian's Villa (Tivoli), it was immediately recognized as that which had been described by the naturalist Pliny. The lovely figure of a **Young Girl with a Dove**, clasping it to her breast as a serpent attacks, symbolizes the human soul choosing between good and evil. The "Room of Venus" contains the **Capitoline Venus**, which was found in the Suburra neighborhood in the 17th century. In the style of Praxiteles, this statue is perhaps the most pleasing representation of all the goddesses; here Venus can be admired in all her beauty, full of charm and grace.

The "Room of the Emperors", contains about eighty busts of Roman Emperors, with a few Empresses; it is the most interesting portrait

Bust of the Capitoline Brutus

gallery in existence.

The "Room of the Philosophers" contains many busts of ancient writers and Greek and Roman warriors. The seated figure at the center of the room is believed to be **M. Claudius Marcellus**, one of the Roman generals of the Second Punic War. Among the many busts, four are of the great epic poet of Greece, **Homer**, traditionally represented as old, poor and blind. **Socrates**, the celebrated Athenian philosopher, is portrayed here

with a flattened nose, thick lips and protruding eyes, like a satyr. The "Room of the Faun", includes, among other works, the **Laughing Satyr**.

The "Room of the Gladiator": in the center of room lays the **Dying Gaul** a marble copy of the bronze statue from the monument at Pergamon. The simple and natural position of the body, the facial features which express deep anguish while revealing human strength blend marvelously to make this statue one of the most significant expressions of Hellenistic culture.

The well-known group of **Amore e Psyche**, an enchanting Hellenistic creation, shows the chaste kiss of young lovers.

The **Satyr Resting** is the best copy of an original in bronze by Praxiteles, the Greek artist who had the divine gifts of tender beauty and grace.

SANTA MARIA IN ARACOELI rises from the highest point of the Capitoline Hill, where there was once the Arx, or citadel of Rome. A legend tells how Augustus raised an altar here to the "Son of God", inspired by an oracle of the Sybil who had foretold of the birth of Jesus.

The "Capitoline Basilica" is noted for its old reliquaries, tombs, fres-

Center, San Giovanni, *by Caravaggio. Below,* Love and Psyche.

coes, gilded ceiling, and ancient relics. Originally it belonged to the Greek monks, but passed to the Benedictines in 883 and finally to the Franciscans in 1250. The main entrance to the church is reached by a **stairway** of 124 steps, built in 1348 as an offering to the Virgin Mary who had liberated the city from a terrible plague and inaugurated by Cola di Rienzo. From the top there is a splendid view of the city. The Romanesque brick **facade**, with traces of mosaics from the late 13th century, was never finished.

The Esquiline Venus.

There is a side entrance to the church from Piazza del Campidoglio. Inside, just above the door, is a beautiful 13th century mosaic of a **Madonna and Child** and two angels. The nave of the church is supported by 22 columns made of various materials, taken from several pagan temples.

The marvelous 16th century gold coffered **ceiling** was constructed to celebrate the victory of Marcantonio Colonna, who in 1571 led the Christian fleet to victory over the Turks in the famous battle of Lepanto. The interesting, Byzantine-style painting of the **Madonna in Aracoeli**, on the high altar, has been attributed to Saint Luke, although scholars date the piece to between the 6th and 11th century.

The richly decorated **ambones**, at the end of the central nave, are by Lorenzo Cosmati and his son Jacopo, whose signature is on the right pulpit (12th century).

In the left transept, the octagonal

The Basilica of Santa Maria in Aracoeli - Inside.

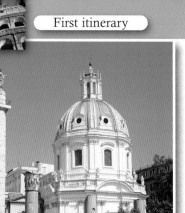

Trajan's Forum. Trajan's Column.

floor, is a white marble altar decorated with sculptures and Cosmatesque mosaics (12th century), that illustrate the Augustan legend as described in the inscription on the table of the altar to St. Helen. The tall, slender statue representing the saint is a contemporary work by Andrea Martini (1972).

PIAZZA VENEZIA takes its name from **Palazzo Venezia**, built in 1455 by the Venetian Pope Paul II (1461-1471), while he was still a cardinal. It was the first great Renaissance palace in Rome, and was richly decorated with outstanding works of art. The structure typifies the early Renaissance period, as it marked the transition to a modern palace from the medieval fortified dwelling, of which it retains certain features.

The **Vittorio Emanuele II Monument** (also called the "Vittoriano"), was designed by Giuseppe Sacconi

chapel dedicated to **St. Helen** marks the place where the altar raised by Augustus once stood. Just under the altar to St. Helen, at a level 15 cm. (6 in.) beneath the

The Vittorio Emanuele II Monument, designed by Sacconi.

Night view of Trajan's Markets.

(1885-1911). It rises from the foot of the Capitol Hill, where it was squeezed into the heart of the city, forever changing the relationship between this hill and its surroundings. The Venetian sculptor Chiaradia worked for twenty years on the equestrian statue of the king, which was completed by Gallori (1901) after the death of the artist. The elaborate bas-reliefs on the base, which represent the most famous Italian cities, were designed by Maccagnani, who for many years collaborated with Sacconi in carving the three-dimensional ornamentation. The building's two colossal **chariots** are surmounted by winged Victories, whose dark bronze contrasts with the white marble and makes them visible against the Roman skyline. They were made by Carlo Fontana and Paolo Bartolini in 1908. In the center is the **Altar of the Fatherland**, crowned by the statue of Rome, at whose feet since 1921 lies the **Tomb of the Unknown Soldier**. *Via*

Trajan's Column.

dei Fori Imperiali begins to the left of the monument, a broad, straight road built in 1932, which takes its name from the ruins of the fora it passes over.

TRAJAN'S FORUM. The Emperor M. Ulpius Trajan was born in Italica (Spain) in 53 B.C. The formidable task of his reign was the expansion of the Empire towards the east, beyond Dacia. The Dacian Prince Decebalus, a true military genius, had imposed an ignominious peace upon the Roman emperor Domitian.

In 101 A.D. Trajan departed for the Danube. Once his roads and fortifications were ready, he took the Dacian capital by force and imposed extremely hard conditions which Decelalus did not want to endure.

In 105 A.D. there was a new battle. The Dacians fought desperately, but their army was destroyed. The heroic prince committed suicide and Trajan returned to Rome

The Vittorio Emanuele II Monument.

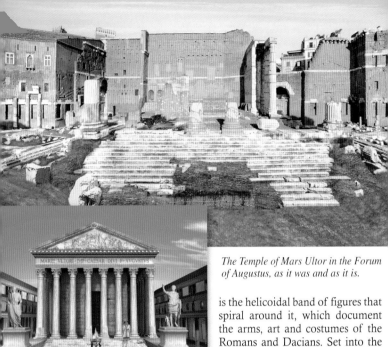

The Temple of Mars Ultor in the Forum of Augustus, as it was and as it is.

laden with treasure. After the celebration of the triumph, Trajan decided to commemorate his victory by building a Forum that would surpass all other fora in splendor and scale. He entrusted the project to the great architect, Apollodorus of Damascus. But the great monument to the victory over the Dacians is the noble **Column**, which after 19 centuries was returned to its original majesty and antique splendor by careful restoration. The ashes of the emperor were once set into the base of the column and his statue once stood on top.

The column consists of 19 blocks of marble and a spiral staircase which leads to the top. The most important part of this historic monument is the helicoidal band of figures that spiral around it, which document the arms, art and costumes of the Romans and Dacians. Set into the Quirinal Hill is the complex known as TRAJAN'S MARKETS, which consists of a well-preserved, semicircular, three story structure, and above, a large vaulted hall, which resembles a basilica. The entrance to the complex is at Largo Magnapoli on Via IV Novembre.

The FORUM OF JULIUS CAESAR, consecrated in 46 B.C. and later finished by Augustus was the first of the so-called Imperial Fora built with the spoils of victory from the Gallic Wars. Formed by a rectangular piazza surrounded on all sides by porticoes, it had at its center the **Temple of Venus Genetrix**.

The Julian family, to which Julius belonged, claimed to originate from Julo, or Ascanius, son of the Trojan hero Aeneas, who according to Homeric mythology was son of the mortal Anchises and the Goddess Venus. The temple featured many

The Forum of Julius Caesar, as it was and as it is.

works of art, among them the sculpture of Venus Genetrix by Arcesilao. In its simplicity the Forum of Julius Caesar surpasses the narrow dimensions of the Republican age, and from an historical point of view, underlines the passage to the imperial age by anticipating the monumental complexes built by Caesar's successors. The Forum was expanded by Trajan, who added the Basilica Argentaria and rededicated the temple, along with Trajan's Column, in May of 113 A.D.

The FORUM OF AUGUSTUS. After the assassination of Caesar, the conspirators Brutus and Cassius went to take possession of the provinces of Syria and Macedonia. In 42 B.C., they led their armies at Philippi against the heirs of Caesar, Octavian and Marc Antony. Just as Julius Caesar took a vow at Farsalo, so Augustus took one at Philippi: in the event of victory, he was to build a temple in a new Forum and dedicate it to Mars, father of the Roman people and God of war. After the victory and the death of the two conspirators, Augustus maintained his vow and built the **Temple of Mars Ultor** (the Avenger) in the center of the new Forum, and inaugurated it on the first of August in the year 2 B.C. Excavations have brought to light magnificent remains of this forum and the gigantic temple, among them three Corinthian columns that once stood 15 meters in height. Augustus was the first Emperor (27 B.C. - 14 A.D.); under his reign, Jesus Christ was born.

The FORUM OF NERVA. Begun under the Emperor Domitian, this Forum was inaugurated in 97 A.D. by his successor Nerva. Built after the Forums of Caesar and Augustus, it was necessary to make the best of

The Colosseum as it was and as it is (pages 18 and 19). ⇨

The inside of the Colosseum as it was in Imperial era and as it looks today.

rather limited space, and so it extended in length rather than width.

This was the site of the **Temple of Minerva**, which was still standing in 1606 when Pope Paul V had it demolished in order to use its marble to build the Pauline Fountain on the Janiculum Hill. New excavations of the Forum of Nerva seek to reconstruct the historical events and architectural history of the area over the centuries.

At the end of the Via dei Fori Imperiali, between the Esquiline, Palatine and Celian Hills, rises one of the greatest wonders of Roman civilization: the **COLOSSEUM**.

This immense amphitheater, whose imposing remains still allow us to admire its ancient splendor, was begun by Vespasian in 72 A.D. and completed by his son Titus in 80 A.D. It was built by Jewish prisoners. It's true name is the "Flavian

Amphitheater", though it was commonly called the Colosseum, both for its proportions and its vicinity to the Colossus of Nero. There is hardly a page of Roman history that is not in some way connected to the Colosseum, which became the symbol of the city and its life.

The Colosseum had the same function as a modern giant stadium, but the favorite spectacles in Roman times were the games of the Circus (ludi circenses), which probably had been invented in the late Republican era, with the intention of cultivating the war-like spirit that had made Romans the conquerors of the world. This was the origin of the professional gladiators, who were trained to fight to the death, while wild beasts of every sort increased the horror of the show. Dion Cassius said that 9000 wild animals were killed in the one hundred days of celebrations which inaugurated the amphitheater. After the animals were killed and removed, the arena was often filled with water in order to stage naval battles. The Colosseum is elliptical in shape, 187 meters at its longest end and 155 meters at its shortest. The height of the external ring reaches 50 meters from ground level. It was designed to accommodate an estimated 55,000 spectators. Around the exterior run three orders of arches, respectively adorned with Doric, Ionian and Corinthian columns, and a fourth floor with Corinthian pilasters. Of the 80 arches that make up the elliptical ring, four correspond to the entrances at the four axes, of which only the entrance of honor reserved for the Emperor remains.

The Colosseum was usually uncovered, but in case of rain it was covered by an immense velarium, which was maneuvered by two squads of sailors belonging to the fleets of Ravenna and Cape Misenum. These two squads also took part in the

Inside of the Colosseum.

The Via Sacra with the Arch of Titus in the background.

naval battles which were often staged in the amphitheater.

When this amphitheater was in its full glory, it must have been a stupendous site of Roman greatness. But even today, after so many centuries, the Colosseum is the pride of Rome and a marvel to its visitors.

Nonetheless the history of the amphitheater is not without long periods of abandon and neglect. The end of the Roman Empire was marked by two earthquakes (in 442 and 508), which caused great damage to the structure. The Colosseum was nonetheless still in use under Theodoric, ruler of the Romano-Barbaric kingdom of the Goths, who in 523 authorized the staging of the *venationes*, the traditional hunt of the wild beasts. From that point began the total abandon that saw the Colosseum used as a cemetery, a fortress, and above all, after the earthquake of 1349, as a quarry for building materials. The marble which once covered it almost entirely was reused in the busy period of construction during the Renaissance. In order to halt the serious decay of the Colosseum, Pope Benedict XIV (1740-1758) consecrated the old amphitheater by setting up a **Way of the Cross** and raising a cross on the site, which has been connected to thousands of Christian martyrs. Though Christians were certainly among the many who were killed here, there is no historical evidence that Christians were ever massacred in the Colosseum.

FORUM ROMANUM

1. *Arch of Septimius Severus*
2. *Rostra*
3. *Column of Phocas*
4. *Temple of Saturn*
5. *Basilica Julia*
6. *Via Sacra*
7. *Basilica Emilia*
8. *Temple of Julius Caesar*
9. *Arch of Augustus*

10. *Temple of Castor and Pollux*
11. *House of the Vestal Virgins*
12. *Temple of Romulus*
13. *Temple of Antoninus
    and Faustina*

14. *Basilica of Maxentius*
15. *Temple of Venus
    and Rome*
16. *Colosseum*
17. *Arch of Titus*

The Temple of Venus and Rome seen from the Colosseum, as it was and as it is.

The Arch of Constantine.

The **Arch of Constantine** was built by the Senate and the Roman people at the edge of the Forum, on the Via Sacra, in memory of the victory over Maxentius at Ponte Milvio in 312. Because it was built largely from pieces from the arches of Trajan and Marcus Aurelius, and from other monuments, this arch was derisively called a "cornacchia di Esopo" (Aesop's Magpie).

Toward Via dei Fori Imperiali is a square foundation of travertine, which marks the spot where the **Colossus of Nero** stood. The famous statue was first erected by Nero in the atrium of his Golden House, and later brought here by the Emperor Hadrian to make room for the exceptional twin **Temple of Venus and Roma** which he had designed himself, was the largest, finest religious building in Rome. The columns have been reconstructed and placed to form the portico that once surrounded the temple. Relics and objects of interest found in excavations of the Forum area are on display in the "Antiquarium Forense," in the nearby convent annex.

The church and the Antiquarium are found inside the **FORO ROMANO** (Roman Forum), the monumental complex whose remains lie between the Capitol Hill, the Imperial Fora, the Colosseum and the Palatine Hill. The center of the civic and economic life in Republican times, the Forum maintained an important role also in the Imperial period.

The Forum was crossed by the **Via Sacra**, which led to the Capitol Hill and also served as the route of the

Arch of Constantine, detail.

Above, the Basilica of Maxentius. Below, the House of the Vestal Virgins.

triumphal processions of victorious generals laden with booty and followed by ranks of prisoners. While the oldest section of the Forum (built in the Republican era) stretched from the opposite side of the valley to the edge of the Capitol Hill, the entrance on the square of the Colosseum leads to the most recently built section, which dates from the Imperial Age. On the Via Sacra, at the top of the Velia, is the **Arch of Titus**, which the Senate built after the Emperor's death in memory of his conquest of Jerusalem (70 A.D.). On the inside of the arch are two fine bas-reliefs: the Emperor on his triumphal chariot and the procession of the Jewish prisoners carrying a seven-branched candelabrum.

The immense **Basilica of Maxentius** (also called the Basilica of Constantine) was the last edifice built in the city which conveys the magnificence of Ancient Rome. It was begun by Maxentius and completed by his successor Constantine. Part of this imposing 4th century structure has been restored, revealing the portion which faced the Forum and the smaller northern aisle. The great

The Temple of Antoninus and Faustina.

apse and powerful barrel vaults were a source of inspiration to Renaissance architects; it is thought that this ruin inspired Bramante's plans for the new St. Peter's.

The **Temple of Antoninus and Faustina** is the best preserved building in the Forum. The loss of Faustina embittered her husband, the Emperor Antonius Pius. After her death, the Emperor wanted to deify her and built a magnificent temple in her honor (141 A.D.). This temple was transformed in the middle ages into the church of "San Lorenzo in Miranda". The round **Temple of Vesta** dates from the time of King Numa Pompilius (8th century B.C.), when it was built to guard the Palladium (the image of Minerva) and other sacred objects brought to Italy by Aeneas, and upon which it was believed the security of the city depended. The six Vestals were chosen from patrician maidens, the daughters of free men, and had to keep the fire burning. They enjoyed special privileges, but if

one broke her vow of chastity, she was buried alive in the Campo Scellerato (Field of Villains). They lived nearby in the **House of the Vestal Virgins**, which was almost totally reconstructed, along with the Temple of Vesta, by the Emperor Septimius Severus after a fire in 191 A.D. Many statues and interesting inscriptions remain. The house, comparable to a modern convent, was divided into different chambers which opened onto the large central atrium.

The **Temple of Julius Caesar**, which Octavian built in memory of his uncle, was begun in 42 B.C. on the spot where the dictator's body was burned, and consecrated in 29 A.D. together with the nearby **Arch of Augustus**, of which only the foundation remains.

The **Temple of Castor and Pollux** (also called the "Temple of the Dioscuri") was built in 484 B.C. to commemorate the victory of Aulus Postumius over the Latins in the battle of Lake Regillus.

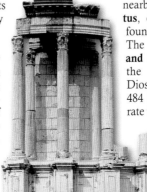

The Temple of Vesta.

The three Corinthian columns and part of the cornice date to the era of Tiberius or Hadrian (1st or 2nd century A.D.).

The **Basilica Julia**, built by Julius Caesar in the middle of the 1st century B.C., was an enormous structure with five naves , divided in sections with movable partitions, which allowed more than one audience to take place at the same time. The **Column of Phocas** was the last classical monument added to the Forum. At the beginning of the 7th century, the Byzantine Emperor Phocas allowed Pope Boniface IV to convert the Pantheon into a Christian church. The column was erected in 608 A.D. by the representative of the Emperor in Rome, by taking a column and base from a pre-existing monument and mounting a bronze statue of the Byzantine Emperor on top.

The **Temple of Saturn** was erected by the Consul Titus Larcius on the 17th of December, B.C. It was always used as the public treasury, and as a repository for the standards of the Legions and the decrees of the Senate. Sacred treasures were held in an underground chamber. The temple was enlarged in 42 B.C., and rebuilt after an fire in the 4th century A.D. Three columns remain of the **Temple of Vespasian** which was built by the son of Domitian in 94 A.D. and later restored by Septimius Severus.

The **Temple of Concord** was built by Furio

The three columns of the Temple of Vespasian (left).

The Roman Forum, center of the city's public life in ancient times.

Camillo, the conqueror of the Gauls in 367 B.C. in memory of the agreement concluded at Monte Sacro between the plebians and patricians. It was in this temple that the Senate gathered to hear the last "Catilinaria" of Cicero (63 B.C.).

The complex, overdone **Arch of Sep-**

View of Roman Forum.

timius Severus points to the coming decline of Roman art. It had been erected in honor of Septimius and his sons, Caracalla and Geta. In the inscription recalls an Imperial tragedy: the murder of Geta by Caracalla, who later had his brother's name removed from the monument. Septimius Severus reigned for 18 years (193-211) and, quite unusually for the 3rd century, died of natural causes.

The **Comitium**, where the representatives of the people gathered for public discussions, had previously been the tribunal. The Comitium consisted of three elements: the *square*, where the popular assembly met, the *Curia*, where the Senate deliberated, and the *rostrum* from which the orators spoke.

The **Rostra**, of which the great platform is still visible, were built by Caesar in 44 B.C., shortly before his death. From this platform the orators and political leaders addressed the people.

The **Curia** was the Forum's first

The area between the Colosseum and Circus Maximus in the Imperial era.

civic center, and consisted of the **Curia-Comitium** complex located between the Basilica Emilia and the Arch of Septimius Severus, which served as meeting place for the Senate, and later as a setting for sacred ceremonies and early gladiator shows.

The **Basilica Emilia** was built by Emilio Lepidus and Fulvius Nobilius in 179 B.C., and subsequently rebuilt and restored many times under the care of the Aemelia family, until a fire at the beginning of the 5th century did irreparable damage. It was one of the greatest buildings in the Forum, used as many others of its kind for the administration and courts of the city.

Another historic Roman hill, the PALATINE, faces the Forum, preserving unforgettable memories in its luxuriant vegetation. The Palatine was the center of Rome in two distinct periods: that of the Roman Kings and of the Empire. During the republic the Palatine was home to patrician families: Quintus Hortensius, the celebrated orator who emulated Cicero, had a house here which later was acquired and enlarged by Augustus. As soon as Augustus became Emperor, he

made his Imperial residence on the Palatine. Subsequently, Tiberius, Caligula, the Flavii and finally Septimius Severus built palaces here.

The Palatine was the cradle of Rome. According to legend, it was on the Palatine that Romulus first traced the square outline of the city, and from then on served as the seat of the Roman Kings. Accordingly, the Palatine was the chosen residence of emperors from Caesar to Septimius Severus. The only exception being Nero; and though he built his great Domus Aurea (Golden House) elsewhere, he never inhabited it.

Thanks to recent excavations, the ruins on this historic hill speak eloquently to the visitor. From atop the Palatine, the unparalleled view, its complex of ruins, and the wisely adapted ornamentation and for the truly stupendous panorama.

The **Clivus Palatinus** leads up to the Palatine, and the stairs on the right to the splendid **Villa Farnese**, with its 16th century Casina and Farnese Gardens, supported by the powerful arches of the **Domus Tiberiana**.

The nearby **House of Livia** is a typical example of a patrician house of the late Republican period which together with the **House of Augustus** and the **Temple of Apollo** formed the Augustean complex, the first Imperial complex on the on the Palatine. The murals, in the Pompeian style, are interesting despite their poor condition. To the right is the **Palace of the Flavii**, designed by Rabirius for the Emperor Domitian. It included a basilica, aula regia and lararium on the left; a peristyle in the center; and a triclinium on the right, which features remains of pavement and two nymphaea, one of which is in very good condition. Attached to the palace was the **Domus Augustana**, where the Imperial court lived.

The **Stadium of Domitian** (160 meters x 48 meters) is surrounded by fragments of porticoes, statues, fountains, and on one side, the large niche of the Imperial loggia. Nearby are the ruins of the **Palace** and the massive **Baths of Septimius Severus**, at the foot of which rose the Septizonium, an imposing building whose remains were demolished by Pope Sixtus V.

The enormous elliptical **Circus Maximus** (664 meters x 123 meters) runs along the base of the Palatiine Hill, almost entirely filling the space between the Palatine and Aventine Hills. The huge basin is still buried. Recent attempts to landscape the barren slopes have not been maintained. In the time of Augustus, the Circus Maximus held 150,000 spectators, and with additions by Trajan, 250,000. The Circus was used for the Roman chariot races, which were among the greatest spectacles for the Roman people.

The Palatine Hill. Rooms in the Domus Augustana and, on the right, the Farnese Gardens. The Circus Maximus and the Imperial Palaces (below).

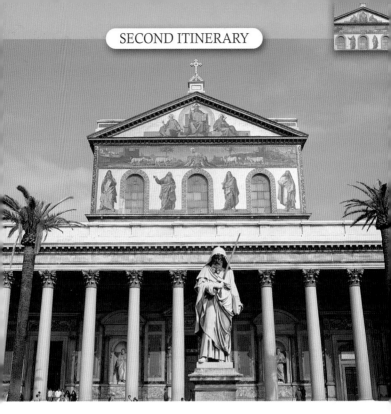

Theater of Marcellus • Isola Tiberina
Forum Boarium • Basilica of San Paolo • EUR

On the left, near the beginning of Via del Teatro Marcello, a rock rises which is thought to be the famous **Rupe Tarpea** (Tarpean Rock), from which the traitor Tarpea was thrown, and subsequently all others punished for betraying Rome.

The fine **Theater of Marcellus** (recently restored) is the only ancient theater left in Rome. It was conceived by Julius Caesar and later built by Augustus in honor of Marcellus, son of his sister Octavia, who died in 23 B.C. at age 20, and was immortalized in the poetry of Virgil.

The original structure accommodated between 15,000 and 20,000 spectators. What remains of the structure, which must have served as a model for the Coloseum, is a part of the curved exterior wall with an elegant double row of Doric and Ionic arches. Above is the 16th century Savelli palace (later of the Orsini) built into the theater by Baldassare Peruzzi.

To the right of Theater of Marcellus rise three columns from the *Temple of Apollo Sosiano* (5th century B.C.). Nearby are the remains of the **Portico di Ottavia** - built by Augustus to honor his sister. The propylaeum serves as the atrium of the 8th century church of **Sant'Angelo in Pescheria**, named for the fish market which was once located on the same site.

A footbridge crosses from the Lun-

The Basilica of St. Paul. In the foreground, the severe statue of St. Paul.

The Isola Tiberina on the Tiber.

gotevere to the **Isola Tiberina** (the island on the Tiber), where the church of **St. Bartholomew** stands on the ruins of the celebrated Temple of Aesculapius, the Greek God of medicine, once a pilgrimage site for the diseased.

Two bridges join the island to the rest of the city: **Ponte Fabricius** (also known as Quattro Capi), built in 62 B.C. and still intact today, and **Ponte Cestio** (46 B.C.). The nearby *Ponte Palatino Bridge* was formerly the site of the **Ponte Sublicio**, not-

ed for the legend of Horace Cocles, the Roman hero who single-handedly fought the Etruscans under Porsenna.

Back across the Ponte Fabricius is the Jewish **Synagogue**, built in 1904 in the Babilonian style, with a gray aluminum cupola. Behind is the Ghetto, a neighborhood where the Jews of Rome were segregated from the 16th to the 19th century, and where many Jews still live.

The Via di Teatro di Marcello leads to Piazza della Bocca della Verità, a

The façade of the Theatre of Marcellus.

site of great religious and commercial importance to pre-Roman settlers of the area, and later as the Roman **Forum Boarium** (cattle market). At the corner of Via Petroselli is the interesting medieval **Casa dei Crescenzi**, built in the 10th century for the powerful Crescenzi family, perhaps as a fort meant to guard the river. It is decorated with fragments from several Roman buildings.

The 1st century B.C. temple named for **Fortuna Virile** is identified with the *Temple of Portunus*, the protector of the nearby port, and offers an excellent example of the Greco-Italic architecture of the Republican era. In 872 A.D., a certain Stefano converted it into a Christian church dedicated to Santa Maria Egiziaca; it was then ceded to the Armenians.

The church of **San Giorgio in Velabro** - named for the marsh (velabro) that once existed here - dates to the 7th century, though the lovely bell-tower and Ionic portico were added in the 12th century. A terrorist bombing in 1993 caused severe damage to the church, which was reopened in 1997 after extensive repairs and restoration.

The **Arch of the Argentari**, a puzzling monument covered with poor reliefs, was built by money-changers and shop-keepers of the Forum Boarium and dedicated to Septimius Severus and Julia Domna, whose portraits are seen on the reliefs. Opposite is the entrance to the Cloaca Maxima, and the **Arch of Janus**, with four faces which date to the time of Constantine. **Santa Maria in Cosmedin**, one of the gems of medieval Rome, stands

The Church of Santa Maria in Cosmedin.

Above, the Jewish Synagogue. Center, the Mouth of Truth.

Above, the Pyramid of Caius Cestius and, on the right, the Temple of Hercules Victor (detail).

on the ruins of a *Temple to Hercules*, visible in the crypt of the church. The suggestive and austere interior is a good example of an early church (8th century). The elegant 12th century **campanile** (bell-tower) is in the Romanesque style. On the left side of the portico is a marble mask called the **Bocca della Verità** (Mouth of Truth): according to legend, a liar who puts his hand in the mouth will have it bitten off. In Roman times the mask covered a drain hole nearby where the Cloaca Maxima flowed into the Tiber.

Roman columns with ancient capitals divide the interior of the church into three naves. The walls of the central nave are decorated with frescoes (8th - 12th century). The *baldacchino* (canopy) is in the Gothic style.

Across from the church is the beautiful 2nd century B.C. **Round Temple**, the oldest Roman temple built of marble that exists today. In the past it was identified as a temple to Vesta, probably due to its resemblance to the temple of the same name in the Roman Forum. The

latest archaeological evidence attributes it to Hercules Victor.

The **Pyramid of Caius Cestius**, at the end of Via Marmorata, was known in the middle ages as the tomb of Romulus. It was actually built in the last years of the Republic to house the ashes of Caius Cestius, who served as praetor, tribune and septemvir of the Epulos, as the two inscriptions attest.

About 2 kilometers down the Via Ostiense is the finest of the churches of Rome, the Basilica of **SAN PAOLO FUORI LE MURA** (St. Paul's Outside the Walls), built over the tomb of the "Apostle of the People." It was the Emperor Constantine who first built a church over St. Paul's tomb. A much larger basilica was built at the end of the 4th century; according to the mosaic inscription on the triumphal arch, it was begun by Theodosius, finished by Onorius, and restored and decorated by Placidias under Pope Leo I (440-461). This splendid basilica, one of the marvels of the world, was destroyed by fire in 1823. It was

Basilica of St. Paul outside the Walls: the interior of the basilica and the cloister by Vassalletto. The Christ Pantocreator. Detail of the mosaic in the apse.

rebuilt by Pope Pius IX in 1854 on the same foundations according to the original design. The magnificent **four-sided portico**, consisting of 150 columns and a majestic statue of St. Paul at the center, immediately suggests a typical Roman basilica. The mosaic **facade** glitters in gold and bright colors. In the portico, among other doors, is a *bronze door* by Antonio Maraini (1930). The inside of the basilica, split into five naves, is opulent and impressive; the eye seems to lose itself in the unending line of columns, among which a mystic light flows from the double row of alabaster windows. Above, the sumptuous Renaissance-style *ceiling* in white and gold, below, the shining marble pavement, and at the end, under the triumphal arch, the lovely *baldacchino* (canopy) in front of the golden mosaics in the apse. Between the windows and the columns is a long series of *medal-*

St. Peter.

lions portraying all the *popes* from St. Peter to Benedict XVI.

On the inner side of the facade, in addition to the two columns which support the cornice, are the *four alabaster columns* which supported the enormous baldacchino by Poletti which covered the ciborio (tabernacle) by Arnolfo di Cambio.

The mosaic on the **triumphal arch** dates to the 5th century, and was ordered by the Empress Galla Placidia. It was placed here after a poor restoration following the fire of 1823.

The Gothic style **canopy**, which stands on four porphyry columns, is a 13th century masterpiece by Arnolfo di Cambio. Under the papal altar is the **marble arch** containing the glorious reliquary of St. Paul. On the right is Vassalletto's **Cosmatesque Cloister** (restored in 1907), which is among the most significant examples of Roman marble work: a genuine masterpiece for its

The Palazzo della Civiltà e del Lavoro is the Eur's most characteristic monument.

Below, the lake in the Eur with, in the background, the Palazzo dello Sport.

fine molding and the richness and elegance of its carvings and mosaics. The **facade** on Via Ostiense and the **bell-tower** are by Luigi Poletti (1850).

Several kilometers further down the Via Ostiense is the **EUR** quarter. Now largely residential, it was originally built to host the World Exposition of 1942, which did not take place because of World War II. Although it has the typical features of fascist architecture, the quarter's urban plan is decisively more pleasant than other sprawling suburban developments which were built on the outskirts of Rome in the fifties and sixties. Worth noting, among other buildings, are the *Palazzo dei Congressi*; the *Palazzo della Civiltà e del Lavoro*; and the well-known *Palazzo dello Sport* (1960) by Pier Luigi Nervi, a brilliantly conceived structure from which extends a beautiful artificial *lake*.

Quirinal • Via Veneto
The Baths of Diocletian • Santa Maria Maggiore

The immense **Quirinal Palace** was begun by Pope Gregory XII in 1574, and served as a residence to the popes until 1870, then to the king of Italy after the declaration of Rome as the nation's capital, and finally to the President of the Republic since 1946. The palace is open to the public on occasion, and inside are works by Bernini, Guido Reni, Maderno and Giulio Romano.

At the center of the piazza is beautiful *fountain* made from a granite basin taken from the Roman Forum and brought here in 1818 by Raffaele Stern, along with an obelisk from the Mausoleum of Augustus and the imposing *statues of Castor and Pollux*. On the right, the elegant and majestic **Palazzo della Consulta**, by Fuga (1732-34).

Down Via del Quirinale is the church of **Sant'Andrea al Quirinale** (1658), a favorite work by Bernini and further down, **San Carlino** by Borromini: a tiny

The Basilica of Santa Maria Maggiore was built by Pope Sixtus III (432 - 440).

43

The Quirinal Palace.
The Helicoidal Staircase at the Quirinal.
Detail of the egyptian obelisk erected on Quirinale Hill.

church and cloister, both full of grace and elegance. Just ahead is the intersection called the *Quattro Fontane* (Four Fountains), with the quadruple background of Porta Pia and the three obelisks on the Esquiline, Quirinal and Pincian hills.

Down Via delle Quattro Fontane is the famous **Palazzo Barberini**,

One of the most famous streets in the world, Via Veneto is known for its elegance.

begun under Pope Urban VIII on designs by Maderno and continued by Borromini and Bernini in 1640. It houses the recently restored **Galleria Nazionale d'Arte Antica**.

Among the many paintings on display, which range from the 13th to the 16th centuries, there are several famous the world over: Raphael's **La Fornarina**, Tintoretto's **Christ and the Adultress**, Caravaggio's **Narcissus** and **Judith cutting the head of Holofernes**. The vault of the great hall of the palace was decorated with **The Triumph of Divine Providence** (1638) by Pietro da Cortona. At the end of the street is Piazza Barberini and Bernini's famous **Fountain of the Triton** (1643).

Diagonally across the piazza is another Bernini fountain, the graceful **Fountain of the Bees**, and the beginning of the famous VIA VENETO.

Just ahead is the church of Santa Maria della Concezione, also known as the Church of Cappuccini, with a painting of **Staint Michael** by Guido Reni and the **Ecstasy of Staint Francis** by Domenichino.

Beneath the church is the macabre **Cemetery of the Cappuccini**, which contains the bones of nearly 4000 friars.

Piazza della Repubblica occupies what was once an esedra of the Baths of Diocletian. At the center of the piazza is the **Fountain of the Naiads**, by Mario Rutelli (1900).

The entire area is dominated by the colossal complex of the BATHS OF DIOCLETIAN, which once extended for over thirteen hectares - far larger than the majestic structure that stands today between Piazza dei Cinquecento and Piazza della Repubblica.

The original plan of the Baths is evident even in the church of **Santa Maria degli Angeli e dei Martiri**, which Michelangelo designed inside the baths, without altering the original Roman structures.

The baths have also been home to the **Museo Nazionale Romano** since 1889. The museum's collection of archaeological relics is one of the greatest in the world, and is also on display in nearby **Palazzo Massimo** (entrance on Largo Villa Peretti) and **Palazzo Altemps** (Piazza Sant'Apollinare, near Piazza Navona).

Piazza della Repubblica with the Fountain of the Naiads.

The Church of St. Mary of the Angels. Below, the Fountain of the Naiads (detail).

The Basilica of SANTA MARIA MAGGIORE is the fourth largest church in Rome and the largest dedicated to the Virgin Mary, and apart from some decorations, is the only basilica to which still retains. preserve its original shape and character.

In August of 356, the Virgin appeared in a dream before Pope Liberius and commanded him to build a church on the site where it would snow the following day. The legend is represented in the medieval mosaics (much restored) in the loggia of the portico. The Basilica, also called "Liberiana", was built in the time of Pope Sixtus III (432-440).

The beautiful **facade**, by Fuga, features a portico with five openings divided by pilasters decorated with columns, and a loggia with three great arches. The Romanesque **campanile** (bell-tower) is the tallest in Rome.

The **interior**, with three naves, is a magnificent sight. At the end of a double row of columns, under the triumphal arch, is the great **baldacchino** (also by Fuga), supported by four splendid porphyry columns. The **ceiling**, by Giuliano Sangallo, was gilded with the first gold brought from America. Along the walls of the architrave, a series of thirty-six mosaics represent **scenes from the Old Testament**, which join the great mosaic of the **triumphal arch,** with scenes from the New Testament. All these mosaics, which date to the 5th century, are of particular importance and beauty. The *pavement* of the basilica is a fine Cosmatesque work of the 12th century.

The **sarcophagus** in front of the high altar was decorated in 1874 by Vespignani, who used the rarest and most precious marble. Behind the metal grill are the celebrated relics of the **Presepio** (crib), con-

Above, Palazzo Altemps, Gaul killing himself.

Baths of Diocletian, Hellenistic Prince.

Palazzo Massimo, Ares Ludovisi.

Above, aerial view of the Basilica of Santa Maria Maggiore.

On the right, the apse mosaic by Jacopo Torriti (13th sec.).

Below, the interior of the Basilica of Santa Maria Maggiore.

sisting of five pieces of the manger in which Christ was put at birth, closed in a silver urn designed by Valadier.

In front is the large kneeling **statue of Pope Pius IX** by Jacometti (1880). On the **high altar**, under the great canopy, a sarcophagus contains the bones of St. Matthew the Evangelist. In the apse with the lancet windows is a fine mosaic of the **Triumph of Mary** by Torriti (1295).

In front of the church rises the beautiful **Corinthian Column** erected by Pope Paul V, who had it brought from the Basilica of Maxentius in the Roman Forum in 1615.

Santa Maria Maggiore. The baldacchino by Ferdinando Fuga (18th sec.)

San Pietro in Vincoli • Oppian Hill
San Clemente • San Giovanni in Laterano

At the intersection of *Via dei Fori Imperiali* and *Via Cavour* is the medieval tower, the **Torre dei Conti**. Up Via Cavour, a stairway on the right (*Scalinata di San Francesco di Paola*) passes through an arch under the **Casa dei Borgia** before reaching *Piazza San Pietro in Vincoli*.

The church of SAN PIETRO IN VINCOLI (St. Peter in Chains) was built under the generosity of an Imperial matron, Eudoxia, daughter of Theodosius the Younger and wife of the Emperor Valentinian III. The chains used

by Herod to hold Peter were sent to Eudoxia by her mother, who had received them from the bishop of Jerusalem. To house the chains, the young Eudoxia built the basilica which was called "Eudoxiana," or more commonly "San Pietro in Vincoli."

The elegant **portico** was built by an architect at the end of the 15th century for Cardinal Giuliano della Rovere, the future Pope Julius II. He ordered Michelangelo to build him a funeral monument, and the first statue by the artist, the **Moses**, is the masterpiece that

The Basilica of San Giovanni in Laterano.

San Pietro in Vincoli. The Mosè, by Michelangelo.

draws most tourists to the basilica. The statue was to be the central figure of an enormous mausoleum which was to have included forty statues. The tomb was instead erected in the right transept under Pope Paul III (1534-49) with only a few statues completed.

Even if the monument falls short of Michelangelo's superb design, the potent sculpture of the biblical prophet is nonetheless among the most moving images of western art. The strong and secure Moses is portrayed in an very simple position, yet emanates a sense of majesty and strength that suggests divine investiture. The two *statues of Rachael and Leah*, which symbolize the active and contemplative life, were also designed by Michelangelo.

The church interior is imposing, the central nave is lined with twenty columns of antique marble. Among the many objects of art in the basilica are the **Tombs of Antonio Pollaiolo** (1432-1498), sculptor, jeweler, painter and engraver, and his brother **Piero**, by Luigi Capponi. The first altar in the right nave is Guercino's masterpiece **Sant'Agostino**. Finally, the 19th century gilded **bronze urn**

The chains are preserved in the bronze urn.

in the reliquary under the high altar, which holds the **Chains of Saint Peter**.

Also deeply venerated are the *relics of the seven Macabee brothers*, held in a paleochristian sarcophagus decorated with episodes from the New Testament, in the crypt.

On COLLE OPPIO (the Oppian Hill) is the access to the ruins of the Nero's celebrated **Domus Aurea**, an imposing, fantastic group of buildings which extended from the Palatine to the Esquiline Hills. Here rose the central palace, ruined in a terrible fire in 104 A.D. The Baths of Trajan, of which few traces remain, were later built on the same site.

The BASILICA DI SAN CLEMENTE, mentioned by Saint Jerome in the 4th century, is among the most interesting churches in Rome from both an artistic and historical point of view. The church was almost buried among the ruins after a terrible fire set by the Normans during a siege in 1084. It was rebuilt in the 12th century by Pope Pasqual II directly above the original basilica, following the same plan, and using whatever architectural elements could be re-used. Despite more recent additions and restructuring, San Clemente remains a rare example of a paleo-Christian basilica. It was not possible to preserve the exact dimensions of the lower church, because the foundations of the right nave had been too severely damaged to allow construction above that area. In fact, in the external wall of the *upper church* are inserted the arches of the colonnade (still visible from the wall near the sacristy) that in the lower basilica had been used to divide the right nave from the large central nave. Consequently, the central and right nave in the upper basilica had to be narrowed,

Domus Aurea. The Octagonal Hall.

Interior of the Basilica of San Clemente.

and leaving the left nave as the only portion which directly corresponds to the lower basilica.

The three naves are separated by two rows of columns, each interrupted by a pilaster. The columns - each different from the others - were probably retrieved from the remains of buildings destroyed by the fire mentioned above.

The most characteristic elements of the upper basilica are the **protiro** (or entry portico) and, inside, the enclosure known as the "schola cantorum", which belonged to the earlier basilica, while the ambones and the twisted candelstick date to the 12th century. The tabernacle and Episcopal chair, at the center of the typical semicircular bench used only by the clergy which runs along the apse, also date from the same period.

The highlight of the basilica is the **apse mosaic**, which represents, in a prodigious synthesis of pagan and Christian figurative elements, the **scene of the Redemption**, a masterpiece of the Roman school of the 12th century.

The *lower basilica*, discovered as a result of excavations in the 19th century, along with other Republican and Imperial structures underneath (among them a Mithraic temple) make this a fascinating archaeological site.

The basilica also features several masterpieces of renaissance art. In the first chapel of the left nave are celebrated *frescoes* by Masolino da Panicale (1431) - once attributed to Masaccio: to the left of the

San Clemente with its dazzling apse. In the center of the nave the Schola Cantorum.

entrance is **St. Christopher**; on the central wall a dramatic **Crucifixion scene**; on the right side wall, episodes from the life of **St. Ambrogio**; on the left side wall, the martyrdom of **St. Catherine** of Alexandria; on the altar, a **Madonna** by Sassoferrato.

On Piazza di San Giovanni in Laterano rises the red granite **Lateran Obelisk**, the tallest of the obelisks which stand today on various piazzas in Rome. It was made in 1449 B.C. by Totmes III and his son Totmes IV of the 18th dynasty of the Pharaohs and brought to Rome in the 4th century, where it was erected on the Circus Maximus. It was then moved here by Fontana for Pope Sixtus V in 1588.

The LATERAN was the residence of the popes until 1309, when the papacy was transferred to Avignon. The palace, called the Patriarchium, was pulled down in 1586 by Domenico Fontana on orders from Pope Sixtus V, who ordered the construction of the current building.

The **Baptistery**, on the piazza, was built by Constantine on the spot once thought to be the site of his baptism by St. Sylvester. It was then rebuilt by Pope Sixtus III (432-440) and subsequently restored several times. Eight porphyry columns which support the cornice of the octagonal structure, while another eight marble columns support the cupola.

On the opposite side of the piazza is the building containing the **Scala**

The interior of the Basilica of San Giovanni in Laterano.

Santa (Holy Staircase), thought to be the same flight of steps which Jesus ascended in the house of Pontius Pilate; it was brought to Rome by the Empress Helena.

The twenty-eight steps may only be ascended kneeling. At the top of the stairs is the private chapel of the popes from the old Patri-archium, called the **Sancta Sanctorum**, richly decorated by the Cosmati family in 1278. On the sides of the stairways are two groups by Iacometti: the **Kiss of Judas** and **Pilate showing Christ to the People** (1854).

SAN GIOVANNI IN LATERANO (St. John in the Lateran), the Cathedral of Rome, was founded by Constantine as the Basilica of the Savior, during the papacy of St. Sylvester (314-335). It was destroyed and rebuilt several times; the current basilica dates to the 17th century.

The imposing facade in travertine was built in 1735 by the architect Alessandro Galilei. The balustrade above the attic holds 15 statues which represent Christ, St. John the Baptist and the Doctors of the Church. In the left side of the por-

tico is a **statue of Constantine** brought from the Imperial Baths at the Quirinal; the **bronze doors** were taken from the Curia in the Roman Forum by Pope Alexander VII (1655-1667). The last door on the right is the *Holy Door*, opened only during holy years.

The **inside** of the basilica, 130 meters long, is divided in five naves by ancient columns which Borromini skillfully incorporated into gigantic **pilasters** in the mid-17th century. In the pilasters he placed a series of statues of the apostles, set into niches framed by green marble columns, thus creating a splendid chromatic contrast of green, gray and white. Above the niches are **high reliefs in stucco** by Algardi (1650), representing *scenes from the Old and New Testaments*. The most striking parts of the interior are the sumptuous gilded **ceiling** in the central nave by Pirro Ligorio (1562) and the **Cosmatesque floor**, under which notable ruins from the Roman period were found.

The vastness of the central nave has as a background an imposing **tabernacle** (late 14th century), dec-

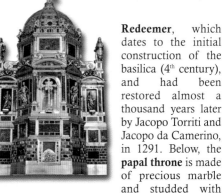

orated by twelve small frescoes attributed to Barna da Siena. Above, the *relics of the heads of Sts. Peter and Paul* are kept in precious silver containers.

Under the tabernacle is the **papal altar** - used only by the pope - made under Pope Urban V in 1367 and restored in 1851. On a bronze **slab** in the crypt is the splendid work of Simone Ghini (1443), brother of Donatello, who *sculpted the prostrate Pope Martin V* with the inscription "temporum suorum felicitas" (the happiness of his times).

The **presbyterium** and the **apse**, at the end of the basilica, are the result of a project carried out by Francesco Vespignani (1884-86) for Pope Leo XIII. Ordered to extend the apse, the artist moved and restored the **Mosaic of the**

Redeemer, which dates to the initial construction of the basilica (4th century), and had been restored almost a thousand years later by Jacopo Torriti and Jacopo da Camerino, in 1291. Below, the **papal throne** is made of precious marble and studded with dazzling mosaics.

In the left transept is the **Altar of the Sacrament**, designed by Olivieri (1592-1604); the four bronze columns had probably been brought from the Campidoglio by Constantine.

Also on the left is a door that leads to the large **Cloister**, a glorious masterpiece of 13th century Cosmatesque art. It was the work of the most famous Roman marble artisans, the Vassalletto family, who were also responsible for the cloister of the Basilica of St. Paul.

San Giovanni. Above, the Tabernacle. Below, the apse mosaic by Iacopo Torriti.

Torre Argentina · Campo de' Fiori
Janiculum Hill · Trastevere

The **Fountain of the Tortoises**, in little Piazza Mattei, is one of the most charming in Rome; its beauty and gracious lines led people to believe that this artistic jewel of the late 16th century had been designed by Raphael. It was actually built by Giacomo della Porta, and the bronzes are by Taddeo Landini (1585). At Largo di Torre Argentina is the **Sacred Area of Largo Argentina**, the most extensive complex from the Republican period that is still visible. The remains of the four temples, which date from the 4th to the 2nd centuries B.C., are not imposing for their size, but interesting for their architectural form and age.

SANT'ANDREA DELLA VALLE was designed by Maderno and built between 1591 and 1650. The cupola is the highest in Rome after St. Peter's, and also one of the most beautiful. The imposing facade, in travertine, is the work of Carlo Rainaldi.

The interior is in the form of a Latin cross, with an spacious nave and large side chapels; the apse, the vault and the cupola combine to give an impression of splendor and solemnity. The Ginnetti-Lancellotti chapel (first on the right) is by Carlo Fontana. The solemn and austere Strozzi (second) is a superb work by Giacomo della Porta, based on designs by Michelangelo. On the altar, the **Pietà** between **Leah** and **Rachael**, is a perfect reproduction in bronze of the noted works by Michelangelo. The four

Campo de' Fiori with its lively daily market.

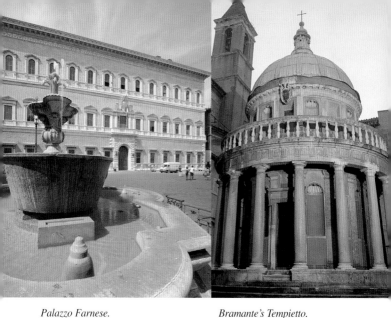

Palazzo Farnese.

Bramante's Tempietto.

tombs in black marble rest members of the Strozzi family.

Campo de' Fiori was for a long time the site of public executions. On February 17th, 1600, the heretic philosopher *Giordano Bruno* was burned here; the monument is the work of Ferrari (1887). The lively market makes this piazza a typical part of Old Rome.

The superb **Palazzo**

Farnese on the piazza of the same name, was begun during the papacy of Paul III by Antonio da Sangallo the Younger (1514), continued by Michelangelo (1546), who added the marvelous cornices, the central window and part of the courtyard, and then completed in 1589 by Giacomo della Porta. This majestic national monument was already the seat of the French embassy when it was ceded to France in 1908.

Ponte Amadeo di Savoia leads to the base of the **Janiculum Hill**, which offers some of the finest views of the city.

Over the undulating sea of roofs, the numerous domes of Rome are silhouetted against the distant backdrop of the mountains, while the Tiber and its turns mark the city's unmistakable shape. On the great panoramic piazza is a **monument to Giuseppe Garibaldi** (1895) by Gallori.

Ahead is the **Paoline Fountain**, built for Pope Paul V by G. Fontana in 1611. The huge semi-

The Fountain of the Tortoises.

The Janiculum Hill.

Paoline Fountain.

circular basin was added in 1690 by Carlo Fontana.

Down on the left is the church of **San Pietro in Montorio**. In the annex to the cloister beside the church, Bramante built a **Tempietto** over the supposed site of the crucifixion of St. Peter. The tiny temple is a masterpiece of the Italian renaissance, charac-

Interior of the Basilica of Santa Maria in Trastevere.

Santa Maria in Trastevere.

terized by the wise use of classical elements such as columns and niches. Via Garibaldi leads from the Janiculum down to **Trastevere**, the "heart of Rome", a quarter where popular traditions are still maintained despite the transformation connected with a certain internationalization of this celebrated part of the city.

A detailed visit to this quarter, rich with old churches and fine buildings, cannot be included as a part of this book due to an obvious lack of space.

Nevertheless, by finishing this itinerary with a stroll through the streets of Trastevere, one can get a good, authentic sense of the old city and perhaps find a typical restaurant, as well.

A brief note only about the oldest basilica in Rome, the church of **Santa Maria in Trastevere**, on the piazza of the same name. Founded by St. Calixtus in 221 and finished by St. Julius in 341, it was rebuilt in the 12th century by Pope Innocent II.

The **facade** was decorated, in the same period, with mosaics and frescoes, and then restored by Pietro Cavallini. In the 18th century, Pope Clement XI had Carlo Fontana build the portico, and Pope Pius IX had the basilica partly restored in 1870.

Inside, the apse is decorated with marvelous mosaics, while between the windows are mosaics which portray the *story of the Virgin Mary* by Cavallini. Beside the facade is the lovely 12th century Romanesque campanile (bell tower) at the top of which is a niche with a mosaic representing a Madonna and Child.

Trevi Fountain • Spanish Steps
Villa Borghese • Foro Italico

Via del **Corso** is the main street of town. At one end of the narrow but imposing street is the obelisk of *Piazza del Popolo*; at the other end, 1500 meters straight down the street, is the *Vittorio Emanuele Monument*; and many papal and princely palaces line the street. The name Corso refers to the horse races held on this road until the end of the 19th century.

Off the Corso, Via delle Muratte leads up to the most sumptuous fountain in Rome: the **TREVI FOUNTAIN**. Legend has it that a foreigner who tosses a coin into the fountain ensures his return to Rome. Set against a large building, the fountain is decorated with bas-reliefs and statues which stand upon mighty rocks from which the water gushes. Spurts and roars animate the impressive scene.

It was Agrippa who brought the Acqua Vergine to Rome in the 1st century B.C., by way of an aqueduct. The fountain was built by

The church of the Trinità dei Monti atop the Spanish Steps.

The Trevi Fountain.

Nicola Salvi (1735) under Pope Clement XII, and was decorated by several followers of Bernini. It is said that the soldiers of Agrippa were in the countryside, looking for water near the Via Collatina, when they came upon a maiden who showed them the source of this pure water; it was from then on called the Acqua Vergine (Virgin water). The bas-relief on the right side of the facade represents this event, the relief on the left shows Agrippa explaining the plan for the aqueduct to Augustus. At the center, the statue of the Ocean God stands on a shell-shaped chariot pulled by winged horses. In 1991 important restoration work was done which returned the fountain to its original splendor.

Halfway down the Corso is Piazza Colonna, with the **Column of Marcus Aurelius**. After the death of the Emperor, the Senate erected a temple and a column in his honor. The column was surmounted by a bronze statue of the Emperor. On the piazza is **Palazzo Chigi**, seat of the Italian Prime Minister. Behind Piazza Colonna is **Palazzo di Montecitorio**, seat of the Italian Chamber of Deputies (parliament). The older portion, once the palace of the Innocenti, was built by Bernini (1653-55), the new portion by Basile (1903-27). Further down Via del Corso, the elegant Via Condotti rises to the right to

Previous page, aerial view of Trevi Fountain.

The Fountain of the Barcaccia.

Piazza di Spagna, and the enchanting **Spanish Steps** (1722). At the top of the steps is the church of the **TRINITÀ DEI MONTI**, with its two cupolas (1495), and an Egyptian obelisk in front, brought here from the Sallustian Gardens in 1789. Inside the church is a fresco of the **Deposition**, a masterpiece by Daniele da Volterra. Nearby, toward the Pincio is the **Villa Medici**, home to the French Accademy.

In Piazza di Spagna, at the foot of the Spanish

The column of Marcus Aurelius and Palazzo Chigi at Piazza Colonna.

Steps, is the graceful **Fountain of the Barcaccia** (leaking boat) by Pietro Bernini. To the right, at the next piazza (Mignanelli) the **Column of the Immaculate Conception** (1856) commemorates the proclamation of the dogma of the immaculate conception of the Virgin Mary.

On the other side of the Corso are Piazza Augusto Imperatore and the **Mausoleum of Augustus**, built for the emperor and his family.

The vast, architecturally superb and perfectly symmetrical **Piazza del Popolo** was designed by Valadier at the beginning of the 19th century. At the center is the second **Obelisk** brought to Rome by Augustus, which was erected here by Fontana during the papacy of Sixtus V.

Piazza del Popolo admired from the terrace of the Pincio gardens.

The church of **Santa Maria del Popolo** is one of the most interesting in Rome. Probably first built in the 11th century, it was completely reconstructed in the early Renaissance. Among the many works of art worthy of attention are: the **Adoration of the Child** by Pinturicchio, above the altar of the first chapel on the right; two mon-

The Temple of Aesculapius (1787) in the ornamental lake of the Villa Borghese gardens.

uments by Sansovino on either side of the high altar: to **Cardinal della Rovere** on the right, and to **Cardinal Sforza** on the left; on the ceiling, the **Coronation of the Virgin** and other frescoes by Pinturicchio. Two paintings by Caravaggio in a chapel in the left transept, **The Crucifixion of St. Peter** and the **Conversion of St. Paul**, are masterpieces by the 17th century artist.

The Chigi Chapel (second on the left nave) was designed by Raphael and is a true gem of the Renaissance. On the altar, the **Nativity of the Virgin** by Sebastiano del Piombo. The church stands at the foot of the **Pincio**, one of the most elegant gardens in the city, also designed by Valadier (1810). The view from the terrace is a magnificent one: in the distance, the Vatican, St. Peter's and Michelangelo's dominate the horizon. The Pincio gardens adjoin one of Rome's most beautiful parks, the VILLA BORGHESE,

The Fountain of the Flaminio obelisk and Santa Maria dei Miracoli (in the background).

built by young Scipione Borghese after he was made a Cardinal when his uncle was elected Pope Paul V in the early 17th century.

On the highest point of the park is the elegant **Casino Borghese**, where Cardinal Scipione Borghese assembled his extremely rich col-

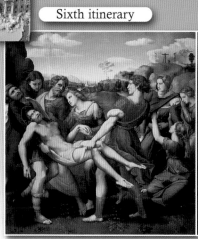

Raphael. Deposition.

Caravaggio. Boy with a basket of fruit.

lection of painting and sculpture. It was built by the Dutch architect Van Zans (Vasanzio) in 1613, and restored in 1782 by Marcantonio Borghese. Toward the end of the 17ᵗʰ century, the great paintings of the collection were transferred to the **Borghese Palace**. About a century later (1807), just as the Casino had been enriched with other classical sculpture by Marcantonio Borghese, it was again impoverished when a great number of its treasures were given, over the protests of the papal government, to the Louvre in Paris by Camillo Borghese (brother-in-law of Napoleon). Francesco Borghese had to then collect still more statues and marble work to bring the collection to its present state.

In 1891 the paintings taken two centuries earlier to the Borghese Palace were returned, and the Casino and the collection were acquired by the Italian government in 1902. The Casino is now home to the **MUSEO e GALLERIA BORGHESE**. The Museo Borghese occupies the ground floor, and includes **Paolina Borghese** (Room I), sister of Napoleon, sculpted by A. Canova. Several famous early works by Bernini (1598-1680) follow: **David with the Slingshot** (Room II), about to hurl a stone at Goliath; **Apollo and Daphne** (Room III), finished by Bernini in 1622, perhaps marks the high

G.L. Bernini.
The Rape of Proserpina *(center).*

A. Canova. Pauline Borghese.

point of his career; The **Rape of Proserpina** (Room IV), which, like the preceding group, was inspired by Ovid; **Aeneas and Anchises** (Sala VI), representing the escape of Aeneas from Troy with his father on his back, followed by the young Ascanius. In Room V the **Sleeping Hermaphrodite** is a copy of an original bronze by Polycle (150 B.C.). The **Egyptian** Room (Room VII) and the Room of the **Dancing Faun** (Room VIII) follow.

The **Galleria Borghese**, on the upper floor, open after a long restoration, contains one of the most interesting collections of painting ever assembled, including masterpieces by Titian, Raphael, Caravaggio and Domenichino.

The Borghese Gallery.

G.L. Bernini. Apollo and Daphne.

ETRUSCAN MUSEUM OF VILLA GIULIA

The Apollo of Veio *(above).*

Etruscan vase.

Sarcophagus of the Married Couple.

Viale delle Belle Arti crosses Villa Borghese, and down on the right is the **Galleria Nazionale d'Arte Moderna**.

The road continues to the **MUSEO ETRUSCO DI VILLA GIULIA**, which since 1889 has been home to a collection of Etruscan artifacts from Lazio, Tuscany and Umbria. The villa was built for Pope Julius III by Vignola in 1553. The thirty-three room exhibit contains important relics including funerary items, such as the **Tomb from the Necropolis of Cerveteri** (575 B.C.), the **Sarcophagus of the Lions**, the **Sarcophagus of the Married Couple** (4th century B.C.) and **Items from the Tomb of the Ambre**; among various objects found in the necropoli are finely decorated terracotta and amphorae, like the **Amphorae Faliscae** of the "painter of dawn" (4th century B.C.) or the famous **biga** from Castro (6th century B.C.); numerous pieces of jewelry, true works of art; of notable interest and impressive size are the statues in terracotta, among them the **Apollo of Veio** and the **Centaur of Nenfra**.

At the end of the road is Via Flaminia, which continues to **Ponte Milvio**, site of a famous battle between Maxentius and Constantine. Just down river is the **Foro Italico**, a modern sports structure, which includes the enormous **Olympic Stadium**.

Santa Maria sopra Minerva • Pantheon
Piazza Navona • Castel Sant'Angelo

The beautiful, large 13th century church of SANTA MARIA SOPRA MINERVA (1280-1290) was designed by the same Domenican friars who built Santa Maria Novella in Florence. With its moderately acute arches supported by high cross-shaped pilasters which divide the naves, this church is a rare example of Gothic architecture in Rome. The name "sopra Minerva" (above Minerva) refers to an ancient temple to Minerva Calcidica, over which the church was built. Under the high altar rests the **body of St. Catherine of Siena** (1347-1380) in a marble sarcophagus. The saint dedicated a great part of her energy to bringing the papacy back from Avignon. After Pope Gregory XI returned the papacy to Rome, St. Catherine retired to the convent adjacent to the church, where she lived her last days. Her letters to kings, popes and others had a great political importance, a spiritual tone, and a high literary value.

To the left of the altar is the famous **statue of Christ Carrying the Cross**, sculpted by Michelangelo between 1514 and 1521. In the left transept is the stone monument of **Brother Giovanni from Fiesole** (1387-1455), one of the great painters of the 15th century in Italy, better known as Beato Angelico. In the chorus are the monumental tombs of the two Medici popes of the Renaissance, Leo X (1513-21) and Clement VII (1523-34) by

Piazza Navona with the church of St. Agnes in Agone in the background.

Antonio da Sangallo the Younger. The **Egyptian Obelisk of Minerva** once stood in front of the ancient Temple of Isis, and was erected in the piazza of the same name by Pope Alexander VII in 1667. Bernini had it mounted on the back of an elephant that was sculpted by Ferrata, one of his best assistants.

The **PANTHEON** - the glory of Rome - is the city's only architecturally intact monument from classical times. Because of the inscription on the cornice of the portico, "*M. Agrippa L.F. Cons. tertium fecit*", for a long time it was believed that the Pantheon, as it stands today, had been built by Agrippa in 27 B.C. and dedicated to the gods of the Julian family; his temple was actually destroyed by a fire in 80 A.D., and completely redesigned by Hadrian. Other restoration was done under Septimius Severus and by Caracalla in the 3rd century.

On March 16, 609 A.D., Pope Boniface IV, with the permission on the Emperor Phocas, changed the pagan temple into a Christian church, bringing the bones of many Christians from the catacombs and dedicating it to "St. Mary of the Martyrs," thus ensuring the preservation of the building to this day.

In 1929 the church, as a result of the Lateran Treaty, assumed the title of the Basilica Palatina, or more properly, the national church of all Italians.

The **portico** has 16 monolithic granite columns. In the tympanum there was once a bronze relief which depicted the Battle of the Gods and the Giants. The ceiling of the portico was covered in bronze, but the precious material, almost 450,000 pounds, was taken down

Santa Maria sopra Minerva. Christ Resurrected by Michelangelo.
The church of Santa Maria sopra Minerva and the lovely square (below).

Section of the Pantheon.

by Pope Urban VIII (1623-1644), and used by Bernini for the baldacchino (canopy) in St. Peter's and other works. In the niches were once statues of Augustus and Agrippa. The **bronze doors** are original.

The **interior** measures 43.4 meters in width and height. Light and air enters through the opening at the top (an oculus, almost 9 meters across, which features some of the original bronze), through which the sky seems to descend to the temple and in turn prayers freely rise to the heavens. The Pantheon's simple

The interior of the Pantheon.

regularity, the beauty of its elements, and its splendid materials combine to give the interior a sublime solemnity.

The **dome** is in reality a cap whose thickness diminishes as it rises. Around the perimeter are seven niches: in the niche opposite the entrance was once a statue to Mars Ultor, who had punished the murderers of Caesar; in the others, statues of Mars and Romulus, Aeneas, Julius Ascanius and of Julius Caesar; other gods and heroes were in the intermediate spaces. The splen-

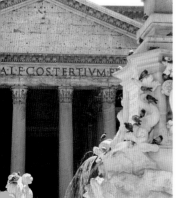

The façade of the Pantheon.

did giallo antico marble columns testify to the temple's original magnificence.

In the first chapel on the left rest the bones of **Perin del Vaga** (1500-47), considered, along with Giulio Romano, as the best of Raphael's assistants. Nearby is the **tomb** of the great painter and architect **Baldassare Peruzzi** (1481-1536). In the second chapel are the **tombs of King Umberto I of Savoy** (1844-1900) and **Queen Margherita** (1851-1926). Between the second and third chapel is a tomb containing the remains of **Raphael** (1483-1520), the most popular among all the painters in the world, whose epigraph says "Here lies Raphael. Living, great Nature feared he might outvie her works, and dying, fears she herself may die."

The **statue of the Madonna** is the work of his assistant, Lorenzetto. Nearby is the **tomb of Maria Bibbiena**, Raphael's fiancé, who died three months before he. Above is the tombstone by **Annibale Caracci** (1560-1609). In the third chapel is the cenotaph of **Cardinal Consalvi** (1755-1824), an exquisite work by Thorwaldsen. In the same chapel, the **tomb of Victor Emanuele II of Savoy**, the first king of Italy (1820-1878). On the altar of the seventh chapel is a 15th century fresco of the **Annunciation** by Melozzo da Forli'.

PIAZZA NAVONA, or Circus Agonale, traces the shape of the Stadium of Domitian, which once occupied this site and held 30,000 spectators. Three magnificent fountains decorate the piazza: In the center - "an Aesop's fable fashioned in marble" - is the **Fountain of the Four Rivers** by Bernini, who designed it as a base for the Egyptian obelisk which was brought here from the Circus of Maxentius. Four figures seated on the rocks represent the Nile, Ganges, Danube and the Rio de la Plata.

The fountain on the south side of the piazza, called the **Fountain of the Moor**, was designed by Giacomo della Porta between 1571 and 1576, but his statues of tritons and masks were later moved to the Giardino del Lago in the Villa Borghese; the statues on the fountain are 19th century copies. The fountain takes its name from the statue of the Moor, which Bernini added in the 17th century. At the north end of the piazza is the **Fountain of the Calderari** (Coppersmiths), so-called because of the many workshops in the area. This fountain also lost some of its original statues and its sculptural decoration was only completed in the 19th century.

The church of **Sant'Agnese in Agone** is a magnificent example of the Baroque style by G. Rainaldi and Borromini. It was built on the site, where according to tradition,

the virgin was stripped naked before being martyred, and miraculously hair grew to cover her body. Underneath the church are remains of a primitive church and the Stadium of Domitian.

Nearby is the majestic **Ponte Sant'Angelo** (once called Ponte Elio), adorned by a double row of *angels* sculpted by followers of Bernini. The bridge was built by Emperor Hadrian (130 A.D.) together with the mausoleum which is now the **CASTEL SANT'ANGELO**. That which seems to be an impregnable fortress was created by the Emperor Hadrian as his tomb. The Mole of Hadrian, or *"Hadrianeum"*, was begun in 123 A.D. and held the remains of the Imperial family until Caracalla (217 A.D.) From what remains it is impossible to understand its original scale; a great

deal of imagination is required to reconstruct the majestic structure. Procopius, the 6th century Byzantine historian, left a description of how the mausoleum appeared in his day: it had a square base, above which rose a great tower decorated by Doric columns, statues and spaces for the epitaphs of the buried. On the top was a colossal bronze group which represented Hadrian on a chariot drawn by four horses; all the walls, of enormous thickness, were covered in Parian marble. It was, together with the Colosseum, the most splendid example of Roman architecture.

The story of the Mausoleum of Hadrian closely follows that of the city of Rome: the struggles and treachery of the Middle Ages, the splendor of the Papal Court and the Renaissance, the horrors of

Piazza Navona is one of the largest squares in Rome.

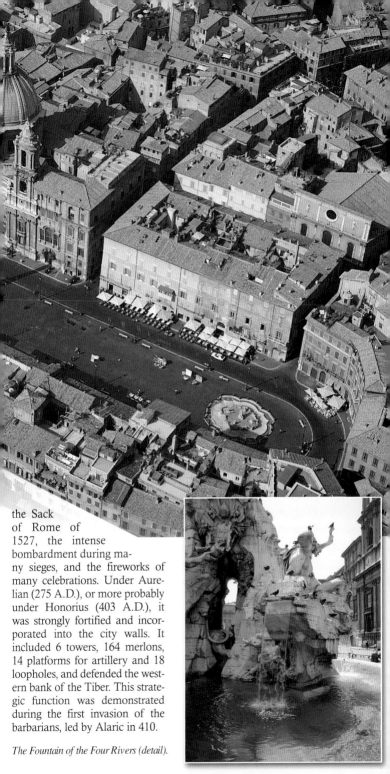

the Sack of Rome of 1527, the intense bombardment during many sieges, and the fireworks of many celebrations. Under Aurelian (275 A.D.), or more probably under Honorius (403 A.D.), it was strongly fortified and incorporated into the city walls. It included 6 towers, 164 merlons, 14 platforms for artillery and 18 loopholes, and defended the western bank of the Tiber. This strategic function was demonstrated during the first invasion of the barbarians, led by Alaric in 410.

The Fountain of the Four Rivers (detail).

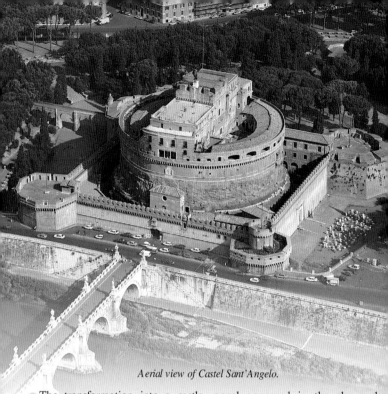

Aerial view of Castel Sant'Angelo.

The transformation into a castle probably occurred in the 10th century, when it became the possession of Alberic and his mother, Marozia, powerful figures in Rome at the time. It then passed to the Crescenzi family and in 1277 was occupied by Pope Nicholas III, who joined it to the Vatican by the famous **passetto** (passageway), a corridor which runs atop the wall that encircles the Vatican. This long fortified passageway allowed the pope to safely walk from the Vatican to the Castle. From that time on the Castle remained under control of the popes, who used it as a fortress and official palace, but also as a prison and place of torture.

The name **Castel Sant'Angelo** dates to the 12th century, but is rooted in a much older legend. During a solemn procession in 590 led by St. Gregory the Great to implore the Virgin to put an end to a plague which was devastating the city, an angel appeared in the sky and landed above the mausoleum, sheathing his sword as a sign of grace granted. A chapel was then built in honor of the angel, followed by a statue which recalled the miracle; eventually the whole building was renamed.

The Castle is steeped in memories of bloodshed and crime, and famous prisoners were held there. In 1527 the city was occupied by invaders led by Carlo V, who besieged in the fortress. From the "passetto", Pope Clement VII witnessed the horrible abuses, theft and sacrilege.

Castel Sant'Angelo can be divided in five floors: First floor (or ground-floor), at which begins the famous 125 meter long helicoidal ramp, a splendid Roman construction. (After the ramp, continue up to the left along the **ramp of Pope Alexander VI** which leads directly to the third floor and the Courtyard of the Angel). Second Floor (or floor of the prisons). It is reached from the Courtyard of Pope Alexander VI on the third floor. Here famous prisoners were once held, such as Arnaldo da Brescia and Benvenuto Cellini; while even more horrid cells - called historic prisons - were reserved for less illustrious guests

Third Floor (or Military Floor). Here there are two great courtyards: the **Courtyard of the Angel**, with the **Marble Angel** by Raffaello da Montelupo in the middle, which stood atop the castle until 1752, and the **Courtyard of Pope Alexander VI** with a lovely 16th century **marble well**. A narrow stairway leads up to the interesting small **Bathroom of Pope Clement VII**, with frescoes by Giulio Romano. In the rooms facing the two courtyards are displays of military paraphernalia from several centuries.

Fourth Floor (or papal floor) with the **Loggia of Pope Julius II**, by Sangallo, at the front of the Castle and the papal apartment composed of magnificent rooms frescoed by Giulio Romano, Perin del Vaga and other followers of Raphael.

The **Treasure Room** or secret archive room, still furnished with wardrobes from the time of Pope Paul III which contained private documents. This room and the one above it formed the burial chamber of Hadrian. The room of the Cagliostra was the prison of the celebrated alchemist of the 18th century.

The **Pauline Room**, or Council Room, decorated by Perin del Vaga (1545) has the richest decorations; on the vault are the frescoes of the deeds of Alexander the Great. On the walls, tromp l'oeil columns separate scenes dedicated to Alexander, Hadrian and the Archangel Michael. Fifth Floor (or last floor) The great terrace offers a magnificent panorama of the city. Above towers the **Bronze Archangel** by Verschaffelt (1753, recently restored).

Hadrian's Mausoleum as it was, today knows as Castel Sant'Angelo.

The Appian Way
Baths of Caracalla • Catacombs

There is no road with more interesting archaeological, artistic and pastoral elements than the **Via Appia Antica** (the Appian Way). Proudly called the "regina viarum" (queen of all roads), it was begun by Appius Claudius in 312 B.C.. Tombs lined the sides of the road for miles, but only members of patrician families, such as the Scipios, Furii, Manili and Sestili were buried here.

The first part of the Appian Way corresponds today to *Via delle Terme di Caracalla* and *Via di Porta San Sebastiano*. The first owes its name to the famous **Baths of Caracalla**, or "Antoniane", which were begun by Septimius Severus in 206 and opened in 217 by Caracalla, and were completed by their successors Helagabalus and Alexander Severus. Lined with basalt, granite and alabaster, the

On the left, Castel sant'Angelo by night. Above the Appian Way.

The Catacombs of St. Sebastian. The three Mausoleums.

enormous baths of hot, warm and cold water could accommodate 1,600 at a time. Splendid vaults, porticoes, esedrae and gymnasiums were decorated with the most precious marble, the most beautiful sculptures and the largest columns imaginable. The ruins of this great complex are still impressive for their size and majesty.

On Via di Porta San Sebastiano, just near the fork in the road, is the **Casina del Cardinale Bessarione**, once home to the renowned humanist of Byzantine origin, who helped spread the cult of classical antiquity in Renaissance Rome. Built in the early 14th century, it was restored by the Cardinal in the middle of the 15th century. Illustrious humanists such as Flavio Biondo, Filelfo, Poggio, Campano, Platina gath-

The Emperor Caracalla.

ered here around the great prelate for erudite discussions about art, science and especially Platonic philosophy. After the death of the Cardinal (1472), the house was abandoned and eventually reduced to a country restaurant. Careful restoration work in 1930 returned this precious architectural gem to its pristine grace.

Nearby is the **Tomb of the Scipios**, which was discovered in the 17th century, and then abandoned until 1926, during which time the portions of greatest archaeological interest were removed. The monument was more complex than its name suggests: it is possible to visit - aside from the sepulcher of the famous family (used from the 3rd century B.C.) - a three story Roman house from the 4th century

A.D. and Christian catacombs.

Just before the Porta di San Sebastiano, the road passes beneath the so-called Arch of Drusus.

The **Porta di San Sebastiano** (once called the Porta Appia) leads out of the *Aurelian Walls*, begun by Aurelian in 271 and finished by Probus in 276. Still in excellent condition, they encircle a large part of the Rome's historic center.

From here begins the most famous tract of the Appian Way, marked by particularly interesting stops, such as the chapel of the **Quo Vadis**, erected on the site where according to legend St. Peter had a vision of Christ. Nero's persecution of the Christians had driven St. Peter to abandon Rome, but a short way outside the city walls, he met another traveler who was walking quickly toward Rome. St. Peter recognized him: "Domine Quo Vadis?" (Oh lord, where are you going?). Jesus responded: "I'm going to Rome to be crucified a second time!"

In front of the Chapel of the Quo Vadis is the circular ruin of the **Tomb of Priscilla**, beloved wife of Abascansius, a freed slave of the court of Domitian (81 - 96 A.D.) who died at a young age, and to whom the poet Cecilius Statius (1st century A.D.) dedicated a poem.

As well as the vestiges of classical Rome, the Appian Way also offers some of the most important evidence about early Christianity. Some of the best-known Roman catacombs, as these ancient Chris-

Aerial view of the Baths of Caracalla.

Catacombs of St. Sebastian.

St. Calixtus. The Crypt of the Popes.

tian subterranean cemeteries have been called since the 9th century, lie beneath the ancient road. The term **Catacomb** (from the Greek katà cymba = near the cavity) actually first referred specifically to the site of the **Catacombs of St. Sebastian**, which was a pozzolana quarry whose galleries were used for the first Christian cemetery.

The catacombs were greatly expanded with the spread of Christianity in Rome; cunicula were carved out on various levels for kilometers, resulting in an inextricable spider web in which it is easy to lose your way. For this reason visits to the catacombs are conducted by official guides from the Franciscan order, who are the caretakers of the cemetery complex.

The Catacombs of St. Sebastian, above which a great basilica was built in the 4th century, were discovered during a 17th century restoration by Flaminio Ponzio and Giovanni Vasanzio. On the second level underground is the **Crypt of St. Sebastian**, where the body of the saint remained until it was transferred to the basilica during the restoration work. The *Cubiculum of Jonah*, with interesting frescoes of the biblical story of Jonah, and the scene of Noah saved from the Ark (late 4th century); the *Sarcophagus of Lot*; the *"Piazzola"*, an early entrance to the catacombs. The *Three Mausoleums* (in particularly good condition) face the Piazzola.

The **Catacombs of St. Calixtus** were the first official burial place for the Christian community in Rome. All the popes of the 3rd century were buried here in the *Papal Crypt*. The first group of crypts was the *Cubiculum of St. Cecilia* (178 A.D.). The statue of the young martyr is by Maderno. After the Crypt of the Popes are the *Cubicula of the Sacraments*, the *Chapel of Pope Gaius*, and the *Crypt of St. Eusebius*.

St. Calixtus. The Crypt of St. Cecilia.

St. Sebastian.

The **Catacombs of Domitilla** are named after the Christian lady to whom this land belonged. She was a member of the Flavians, an Imperial family. There are possibly the most extensive catacombs in Rome. In this area stands the 4th century *Basilica of Sts. Nereus and Achilleus*, which was discovered in 1874 and subsequently restored.

Opposite the Catacombs of St. Sebastian is the **Villa of Maxentius**. Built in the early 4th century, it was immediately used as an imperial residence, but for only a few years. After the victory of Constantine over Maxentius (312 A.D.) and the transfer of the capital of the Empire to the "New Rome" at Constantinople, the Villa was ceded to the Christian church. Today it appears to be a large and well-excavated *archaeological site. Among the ruins is the Tomb of Romulus,* son of Maxentius, who died at a young age; the splendid, well-preserved Circus which once held 10,000 spectators; and finally, built over a country villa that dated to the 2nd century B.C., the *Imperial Palace* with three apses, two nymphea from the first imperial period, and a thermal complex.

The **Tomb of Cecilia Metella** (circa 50 B.C.) stands solemnly on the Appian Way. Cecilia was the wife of Licinius Crassus, son of Crassus the triumvir, who ruled Rome along with Caesar and Pompey and put an end to the Republican era, making way for the Empire (1st century A.D.). The original commemorative marble tablet remains inside the tomb, which

Bas relief of a sarcophagus.

was transformed into a fortress in the middle ages. From here to the fourth mile, the Via Appia Antica remains as it has been since the mid-19th century, when Luigi Canina redesigned it as a romantic road, lined by ancient tombs (mostly restored).

Continuing to the fifth mile, after passing many monumental tombs, is the grand **Villa dei Quintili** (2nd century A.D.). It was once the country residence of the Quintilii brothers, Condianus and Maximus, who both served as Consuls, but was then confiscated by the Emperor Commodus, who transformed it into an lavish country palace. Though it was transformed into a fortress in the middle ages, the baths, a hippodrome, residences and gardens of the older structure are still visible.

Between the Via Ardeatina and Via delle Sette Chiese, not far from the Catacombs of San Sebastiano, is another site of martyrdom: the **Ardeatine Caves**. Just as the first Christians were innocent victims because of their heroic faith, so in this almost deserted place, at sunrise on March 24, 1944, 335 Italians, many of them Jews, fell victim to an inhuman Nazi vendetta. Today, a simple and solemn crypt holds the 335 bodies, lined up in death as in martyrdom.

Porta San Sebastiano.

The Vatican City

The **VATICAN** has been the residence of the popes only since 1377, six centuries interrupted by long stays at the Quirinal Palace. Before the pontifical court was transferred to Avignon (1309-1377), the headquarters of the pope had been at the Lateran. Since then, there has not been a pope who has failed to contribute to the grandeur and dignity of the Vatican, to make this holy hill an increasingly worthy seat for the Supreme Head of the Catholic Church. An uninterrupted succession of 265 men have sat on St. Peter's throne, many of whom were martyrs and saints. The Vatican has been an independent state (called the **Vatican City**) since February 11, 1929, when the Lateran Treaty definitively resolved the "Roman Issue" between the Church and the Italian State.

In Roman times, the Vatican was the site of the great Circus of Nero, where under Nero, St. Peter was crucified (circa 64 - 67 A.D.). His body was buried nearby, more than 250 years later, Constantine built a magnificent basilica on the spot, which was destined to become one of the marvels of the world. During the 73 years that the papacy was in Avignon, the already old basilica was so neglected that restoration was impossible. Pope Nicolas V (1447-1455) decided to rebuild it, and gave the project to Rossellino, but after the pope's death, all work was suspended. It was Pope Julius II

St. Peter's Basilica in the Vatican.

(1503-1513) who began the construction of a new basilica, entrusting Bramante with the design of the great architectural project, which took 176 years to complete.

Until Michelangelo, then almost seventy years old, began to build the dome, there had been a succession of various architects, among them Raphael and Antonio da Sangallo the Younger, and different plans. After Michelangelo's death, the work went on according to his designs, which called for Bramante's original Greek cross plan, but under the papacy of Paul V (1605-1621), Maderno decisively adopted a Latin cross design for the new basilica.

The greatest church in Christendom, **ST. PETER'S BASILICA**, rises on the grandiose **St. Peter's Square**. Michelangelo's mighty silver-blue dome dominates the scene, blending into the sky above, conveying a sense of the absolute and infinite, which touches the soul of all who gaze upon it. The construction of the dome proceeded through problems and obstacles of every kind. Michelangelo was already quite old when he began the

St. Peter's Basilica with the Vatican Palaces.

project in 1546, and when he died in 1564 only the drum had been completed. The rest of the work was finished between 1588 and 1589 by Giacomo della Porta and Domenico Fontana. The **Colonnade** is Bernini's most beautiful work, and forms the solemn entrance to St. Peter's and the Vatican. The two great open semicircular wings seem as if they were the outstretched arms of the church, receiving all of mankind in one universal embrace. If some of Bernini other works appear to be extravagant, this colonnade shows the height of his genius. He also designed the 140 *statues of saints* in which decorate the colonnade, which were sculpted with the help of his pupils.

Pope Sixtus V (1585-1590) chose Domenico Fontana to oversee the erection of the **Obelisk** in the middle of the piazza, a considerable task which aroused wonder and great enthusiasm in the people. The obelisk measures more than 25 meters in height and was brought from the nearby ruins of the Circus of Nero.

The **two fountains**, the one on the right designed by Maderno (1613) and the one on the left by Carlo Fontana (1675), harmonize beautifully with the vast square.

The Borghese Pope Paul V commissioned Maderno (1607-1614) to construct the broad **façade** of

Carlo Fontana's fountain on St. Peter's Square.

the church, and had his name and title written in very large letters across the entablature.

The **Loggia of the Benediction**, above the central entrance, is used to proclaim the election of a new pope, and it is from here that he delivers his first blessing, "Urbi et Orbi" (to the city and the world). Inside the **portico**, above the principal entrance, is the famous mosaic of the **Navicella** (little boat), designed for the old basilica by Giotto during the first Holy Year (1300), which has undergone considerable restoration. Five doors open onto the portico, corresponding to the five aisles in the basilica.

The first door on the left is the **Door of Death** by Manzu', which shows the death of Jesus and that of the Madonna, the death of Pope John XXIII and death in space (1952-1964).

The **Bronze Door**, in the center came from the old basilica; it was designed by Filarete as an imitation of the doors by Ghiberti in Florence.

The **Holy Door** on the far right is only opened every twenty-five years, at the beginning of the Holy Year. On Christmas Eve, the Pope, according to a special ritual, makes a solemn procession to this door, and after a triple genuflection and three strokes of a hammer, the wall is removed and the Pope is the first to cross the threshold and enter the basilica. At the end of the Holy Year the door is re-closed with a solemn ceremony. The modern reliefs which decorate the door are the work of Vico Consorti.

St. Peter's Basilica illuminated.

Another two contemporary doors complete the portico: the **Door of Good** and **Evil** by Minguzzi and the **Door of the Sacraments** by Crocetti.

Entering the church, one is struck by the enormity of the basilica. The numbers speak eloquently: the length of the interior of the basilica, as shown in an inscription in the pavement near the bronze door, is 186.36 meters (the external length, including the portico, is 211.5 meters). Other signs in the floor indicate the lengths of the major churches in the world; the vault is 44 meters high; the dome, measured from the inside, measures 119 meters, with the lantern adding another 17 meters; the perimeter of one of the four piers which support the dome measures 71 meters.

At the end of the immense central nave rises the bronze baldacchino (canopy) which covers the high altar - its 29 meters makes it 4 meters taller than the obelisk on the piazza. Near the transept is the celebrated 13th century **bronze statue of St. Peter**, set against one of the enormous pilasters which supports Michelangelo's dome. In the niches at the bases of the pilasters are four statues: **San Longino** by Bernini, the **Empress St. Helena** by Andrea Bolgi, **St. Veronica** by Francesco Mochi, and **St. Andrea** by Francois Duquesnoy. The high altar, under the cupola, rises above the **Tomb of St. Peter**, which was definitively identified after excavations in the 1950's. In front of the tomb, ninety-nine lamps burn day and night; opposite is the **crypt**, designed by Maderno, rich with

The inside wiew of the dome and the Bernini's baldacchino (canopy).

The Statue and the Tomb of St. Peter.

inlaid marble. Above the altar rises Bernini's fantastic **baldacchino** (1633), supported by four spiral columns, made from bronze taken from the Pantheon. But the glorification of the tomb of the humble fisherman from the Galilee is the majestic **dome** that soars toward the heavens. In the Tribune, four Doctors of the Church support the **Throne of St. Peter**, a stunning work in gilded bronze by Bernini.

Returning toward the entrance, in the first chapel of the right nave is Michelangelo's **Pietà**, sculpted between 1498 and 1499. The artist's name is engraved on the sash that crosses the bust of the Virgin. The next **Chapel of Saint Sebastian** is so called for the mosaic with which it is decorated reproducing the *Martyrdom of Saint Sebastian*, taken from an altar-piece by Domenichino. The chapel contains the **Tomb of Blessed John Paul II**, who was entombed here after his beatification ceremony on 1 May 2011 when his body was moved from the Vatican Grottoes

Chapel of Saint Sebastian, the Tomb of Blessed John Paul II.

where it was laid to rest in 2005. Among the numerous monuments set on the pilasters are Carlo Fontana's *monument to Christina of Sweden*; Bernini's *monument to Matilde di Canossa* (1635) and Canova's *monuments to Pope Clement XIII*, to *Pope Urban VIII* and to the last Stuarts. Bernini's *tabernacle* is in the *Chapel of the Sacrament*.

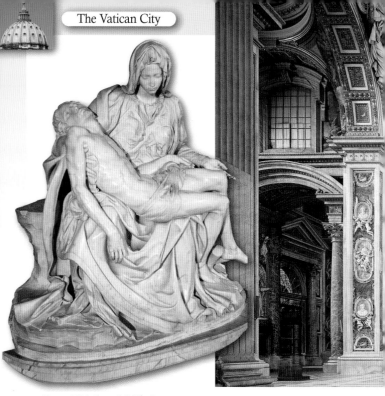

Above, Michelangelo's Pietà

THE SACRED GROTTOES

The lower level of the present basilica, which roughly corresponds to the level of the old basilica which Constantine built, is of particular interest. Excavations under the tomb of St. Peter led to the important discovery that Pope Paul VI announced on June 26, 1968: "The relics of Peter have been identified in a way which we may consider convincing."

Here we find the **Tomb of St. Peter**, the spiritual centre of the Vatican Grottoes located in the so-called **New Grottoes**: in reality it is the oldest part, but its name comes from the fact that it was arranged later. Four oratories open onto the Gallery and several chapels, in two of which are the

The interior of St. Peter's Basilica.   St. Peter preaching to the Romains (IV sec.).

tombs of Pope Pius XII and Pope John Paul I. At the end of the hall are the Old Grottoes, which extend across the vast space under the central nave of the upper basilica. They were made by Antonio da Sangallo the Younger as an interspace to protect the flooring of the new basilica from humidity. In the fascinating shadows cast between the three aisles with the low vaulted ceiling and two rows of sturdy pillars are the funeral monuments of about twenty popes - among them Pope Paul VI, Pope John Paul I, an emperor, a king, two queens, numerous cardinals and bishops, as well as precious works of art and relics from the old basilica. The obligatory itinerary allows for looking around the whole vast area that is visually connected to the **Old Grottoes** extending under the main nave of the Basilica above. The underground area was designed by Antonio da Sangallo as a cavity wall to protect the floors of the new building from humidity.

Panoramic view from the dome of St. Peter's.

THE WAY UP TO THE DOME

Access to the dome is via the right side of the portico. The first part of the ascent, from ground level to the terrace above the central nave (at the base of the dome), can be made on foot or by elevator.

The view from the balustrade is fantastic: Bernini's colonnade in the foreground, the scintillating Tiber a bit further out, and the rest of the city in the distance all create a very harmonious scene.

Passing to the interior, the gallery which runs along the drum of the dome, 53 meters above the basilica floor offers impressive views: Bernini's baldacchino, which is as tall as a building, looks to be a small scale model.

The last part of the climb goes between the two superimposed round vaults which make up the dome, which curve little by little as they rise to the top.

A circular balcony from the lantern looks out onto the unforgettable panorama of the Eternal City.

Descending to the basilica, the **Treasury**, near the Monument to Pope Pius VIII in the left nave, is worth a visit.

The dome of St. Peter's.

THE VATICAN MUSEUMS

The Vatican Museums are exceptionally important because of the richness and prestige of the masterpieces brought together under various popes over the centuries, as well as for their sumptuous setting. The museums are made up of a group of grand buildings and countless rooms, salons, museums, galleries, libraries, chapels, corridors, courtyards and gardens rich with art treasures of every type.

From the Renaissance on, there was not a great artist who did not leave the immortal mark of his genius here.

The entrance to the Vatican Museums is on Viale del Vaticano (see the map - Ninth Itinerary).

The Gallery of the Candelabra.

CHIARAMONTI MUSEUM

This museum was founded by Pope Pius VII Chiaramonti (1800-1823) and is made up of the *Corridor, Lapidary Gallery*, and the *Braccio Nuovo* (New Wing), all in neoclassical style. The Corridor is flanked by statues, busts, sarcophagi, reliefs, etc. - in all about eight hundred Greco-Roman works; the Lapidary Gallery holds more than 5000 pagan and Christian inscriptions. In the Braccio Nuovo is the **statue of Augustus**, found in 1863. After the battle of Actium, Augustus brought an immense amount of Egyptian treasures to Rome, among them the colossal group of **The Nile**.

The Augustus of Prima Porta statue, which dates from between 14 and 29 A D.

MUSEO PIO CLEMENTINO

The Museo Pio Clementino takes its name from its great and generous founders, Popes Clement XIV and Pius VI, who lived between the 18th and 19th centuries.

Across a vestibule is the **Gabinetto dell'Apoxiomenos**. At the center is the athlete from Lysippos (Apoxyomenos), a marble copy of a bronze original that Agrippa brought from Greece. In the Octagonal Courtyard of the Belvedere, classical statues are displayed in four gabinetti (recesses): **Gabinetto del Laocoonte** - The exceptional Laocoon group was dis-

Hermès.

covered among the ruins of the Baths of Titus in 1506. **Gabinetto dell'Apollo** - The statue of Apollo was found in Grottaferrata during the papacy of Julius II, who acquired it for the Vatican. **Gabinetto del Perseo** - It contains the only three modern works on the courtyard: **Perseus with the head of Medusa** and the **two boxers Creugas and Damoxenes**, all by Antonio Canova (1757-1822).

Gabinetto dell'Hermes - The statue of Hermes is a copy of a 4th century B.C. original by Praxiteles.

The **Animal Room** contains reproductions of a great number of animals in marble and alabaster. Of particular interest is the statue of **Meleager**.

The **Gallery of the Statues** contains many important works, including the **Apollo Sauroctonos**, which is copy of a work by Praxiteles, and the **Sleeping Ariadne**, from the Hellenistic period. The **Gallery of the Busts** follow, made

The Laocoon *(1st century B.C.).*

The Vatican Library.

up mostly of Roman portraits. The bust of the young **Augustus** is the highlight of the gallery.

In the **Gabinetto delle Maschere** (Mask Room) are the gracious statue of **Aphrodite** and the well-known **Venus of Knidos**, perhaps the most beautiful of all Greek sculptures.

The **Sala delle Muse** (Hall of the Muses) is decorated with Corinthian Columns, and busts and statues of mythological figures. In the center of the room is the famous statue (1st century B.C.) of the **Torso**, signed by the Athenian Apollonius. In the **Sala Rotonda** (Circular Hall), the magnificent **porphyry vase**, four meters in diameter, is without doubt the richest and most sumptuous piece in this gallery. The **pavement mosaic** was found at Otricoli, and the colossal statue of **Antinous** was brought from Palestrina. The **Hall of the Greek Cross**, houses **two porphyry sarcophagi** which contain the bodies of St. Helena and St. Constance, daughter of the emperor Constantine.

THE LIBRARY

The "Vatican Library" is the most important in Europe for the antiquity and richness of manuscripts and rare books. Several examples are on display in the sumptuous Sala Sistina, including the Codex of the *Bible* from the 4th century; four examples of Virgil from the 3rd to the 5th century; the *Gospel of Matthew* of the 6th century; the famous palimpsest containing a large part of *De Repubblica* by Cicero. This 5th century manuscript was scraped in the 7th century in order to be reused for the commentary "Super Psalmos" by St. Augustine, written here and restored to its original condition in the 9th century.

At the back of the library, in a room on the right, is a precious collection of ancient frescoes among which the most important is the **Aldobrandini Wedding** (from the Augustan period), which represents the preparations for the wedding between Alexander the Great and Rossana.

THE RAPHAEL STANZE

As soon as he came to Rome, Raphael was introduced to Pope Julius II by Bramante. Some rooms above the Borgia Apartment had already been frescoed by Perugino and others, but Julius decided to have them scraped and painted again by the young Raphael.

The first Stanza, called the *Sala di Costantino*, represents the legendary life of Constantine. The frescoes were executed according to Raphael's designs after his death. The first fresco, The **Apparition of the Cross**, represents Constantine's defeat of Massenzio (312) and was painted by Giulio Romano just after the death of the master.

The second Stanza (*Stanza d'Eliodoro*) was painted in 1511-14; its name comes from the fresco which represents the **Chastisement of Heliodorus**. The spirit of the subject in the room was intended to glorify the papacy. Above the window is the scene of the **Miracle at Bolsena**, where in 1264 the real presence of Christ in the Eucharist was proved to a doubting priest by a miracle.

The **Liberation of St. Peter from prison** was skillfully set around the window with the three different qualities of light particularly well portrayed. The **Meeting of Attila** is an allusion to battles with France.

In the third Stanza is Raphael's first work, the **Dispute of the Holy Sacrament**, finished in 1509. The subject of this wonderful fresco is the glory of the Eucharist.

On the opposite wall is the **School of Athens**, representing the celebration of reason, which

The Raphael Stanze. The School of Atens.

The Raphael Stanze. Dispute of the Holy Sacrament.

contrasts to the exaltation of faith on the opposite wall. Above the window is Mount **Parnassus**, the mythic Greek mountain of the gods.

The last Stanza, with frescoes painted by Raphael and his followers during the papacy of Leo (1514-17) is named after the fresco entitled **Fire in the Borgo**. It represents the fire in the city that was miraculously extinguished by Pope Leo IV.

The Raphael Stanze.
The Liberation of St. Peter from prison.

The Sistine Chapel.

THE SISTINE CHAPEL

Between 1475 and 1483, Sixtus IV commissioned Giovanni de' Dolci to build the **Sistine Chapel**. He wanted this essential building to be architecturally isolated, virtually inaccessible from the exterior, as it were fortified.

Its decoration was begun in 1482 and it transformed the severe, almost bare chapel into a precious picture gallery of 15th- and 16th-century Italian Renaissance painting. It was Pope Sixtus IV himself who commissioned some of the best painters of the time such as Perugino, Botticelli, Ghirlandaio and Cosimo Rosselli to illustrate the parallel narratives of the Old and New Testaments which face one another on the central strip of both walls. The **Life of Moses** (Old Testament) on one side and the **Life of Christ** (New Testament) opposite, were therefore painted parallel to one another on the two lateral walls.

Thus **The Journey of Moses**, attributed to Pinturicchio, corresponds on the opposite side to the **Baptism of Jesus** which was certainly painted by Pinturicchio; in addition to the classical Christian symbolism, Roman monuments can be recognized on the hills in the background.

The next pictures are the work of Botticelli: the biblical series on the left includes **Moses with Jethro's daughters**, and in the Gospel sequence on the right, **The Temptation of Christ** and **The Healing of the Leper**.

Continuing, the **Crossing of the Red Sea** by Cosimo Rosselli, is an allegorical glorification of the great victory of the papal troops of Sixtus IV over the Neapolitans at Campomorte (1482), on the side dedicated to he Old Testament. Opposite is **The Calling of the first Apostles**, by Ghirlandaio, Michelangelo's master.

Next in the sequence on one side is **Moses receiving the Tablets of the Law**, which he broke after realizing that the people of Israel were dancing round the golden calf in adoration, and on the other, **The Sermon on the Mount**, both by Rosselli.

The biblical episode of **Korah, Dathan and Abiram** is another work by Botticelli, facing **The Delivery of the Keys to Saint Peter**, painted by Perugino, Raphael's master.

On the left at the end of the series of frescoes on the lateral walls we find **The Testament** and **Death of Moses** by Luca Signorelli, while on the right is one of Cosimo Roselli's greatest works, **The Last Supper**.

A religious ceremony in the Sistine Chapel with the Pope and Cardinals.

THE SISTINE CHAPEL

1) *Separation of Light and Darkness.*
2) *Creation of the Sun, the Moon and plants.*
3) *Separation of the earth and the water.*
4) *Creation of Adam.*
5) *Creation of Eva.*
6) *Original Sin.*
7) *Noah's Sacrifice.*
8) *Noah's Flood.*
9) *Drunkenness of Noah.*
10) *Gioele.*
11) *Eritrean Sybil.*
12) *Ezechiele.*
13) *Persian Sybil.*
14) *Geremia.*
15) *Libyan Sybil.*
16) *Daniele.*
17) *Cuman Sybil.*
18) *Isaia.*
19) *Delphic Sybil.*

In 1508, Julius II, ever eager for new enterprises, ordered the young Michelangelo to paint the **ceiling** of the Sistine Chapel. The gigantic work began in May 1508 and was completed on All Souls Day 1512.

The immense challenge posed by the vast size of the surface of the vault to be covered (an area of at least 800 square meters) and its bareness was brilliantly overcome by Michelangelo with an ingenuity that reveals the rich complexity of his artistic genius. In fact, he covered the actual architecture by painting over it an architectural structure in which he set the various figurative elements with an amazing three-dimensional effect.

The artist incomparably combined painting, sculpture and architecture, making the most of the curves of the vault to fit his powerful figures into the scenes.

In the center of the complex design are a sequence of nine panels showing *Episodes from Genesis*, from the main altar to the entrance wall. They are flanked by the famous *ignudi* (nudes) and portray respectively: the **Separation of Light and Darkness**, the **Creation of the Sun, the Moon and plants**; the **Separation of earth and water**; the **Creation of Adam**. This is the central scene of the cycle, also from the pictorial point of view. The artist expresses the sublime act of creation by the simple touch of finger tips through which a real charge of vitality seems to flow from the Creator to Adam. The **Creation of Eve** and the **Fall** follow original sin is a scene divided into two parts by the tree around which is coiled the serpent with the bust of a woman; twisting to the left, she invites Adam and Eve to pick the forbidden fruit.

On the right, cause and effect are visibly related in the drama of the expulsion from the Garden of Eden.

Outside the scene of earthly paradise, is **Noah's Sacrifice**. This episodes celebrates his gratitude after surviving the catastrophe and is chronologically later than the following scene of the Flood, a harmonious panel thronged

Above lunette with The Ancestor of Christ. *Center the* Prophet Isaiah.

with figures and episodes. Lastly, the **Drunkenness of Noah** ends the powerful sequence on the vault on a note of bitter pessimism about the wretchedness of human nature.

The **Prophets and Sybils** between the triangular spaces at the curve of the vault are the largest figures in this monumental work; they are seated on solemn high-backed chairs and accompanied by angels and cherubs. **Jesus' Forefathers** are shown in the lunettes above the windows and in the triangular "spandrels", while the four corner spandrels are painted with particularly dramatic **Episodes from the Old Testament**, concerning the salvation of the people of Israel.

A good 23 years passed, during which the Christian world was torn apart by the Lutheran Reformation and Rome suffered the terrible Sack of 1527, before Michelangelo painted the **Last Judgement** on the wall behind the main altar. This unique masterpiece is overwhelming and dominated by the splendid audacity of its author who put his whole self into it.

The Last Judgement, a compendium of the Divine Comedy and the pictorial explosion of the "Dies irae", commissioned by Pope Paul II, was begun by Michelangelo in 1535 and completed in 1541. Three hundred figures swarm in a composition which has an amazing coherence and clarity and in which space is organized into a real architectural structure of figures. Christ, the implacable judge, dominates this grandiose scene, his right arm raised in the act of condemnation. His words, "Depart from me, you cursed!" are not spoken, are not written, but they are tangibly felt.

The Virgin beside him is the ever-living link between Christ and humanity. The other figures in the judgement are the prophets, apostles and the martyrs. On the Messiah's right are the elect; on his left, the damned.

Between the two lunettes, hosts of angels in heaven bring the symbols of the Passion. Below, on the left, is the scene of the resurrection of the dead: a group of angels

Above lunette with The Ancestor of Christ. Center the Eritrean Sybil.

Sistine Chapel. The Last Judgement *by Michelangelo.*

in the center, bearing the Book of Judgement, blow trumpets, while the dead stir from gaping tombs to find themselves in the Valley of Jehoshaphat.

As the good rise to heaven amidst the impotent rage of demons, the wicked are precipitated into the abysses where Charon shoves them out of his boat and Minos, the judge of hell awaits them.

Between 1980 and 1994 a large-scale restoration of the frescoes on the ceiling and the Last Judgement was carried out and attracted keen attention all over the world. In fact, by dissolving the heavy layers of dust and lamp-black deposited on the painting with the passing of centuries and the clumsy attempts at restoration with animal glues in the 17th century, somewhat unexpectedly this in-depth cleansing brought the most brilliant colors to light, which has led some experts to revise the theory of the prevalence of drawing over the use of color in Michelangelo's painting.

The section of the Vatican Museums which houses the Vatican Picture Gallery built in 1932.

THE VATICAN PICTURE GALLERY

The pictures exposed in the Vatican Picture Gallery are of exceptional interest: they are part of a collection begun by Pope Pius VI (1775-1799) which underwent various removals before being worthily housed in this functional building. Today the Picture Gallery contains about five hundred works between pictures and tapestries, arranged in the fifteen rooms which compose it according to chronological order: from the Byzantines and early Italians of 1100-1300, whose works are exposed in the 1st room, we arrive, in fact, to the artists of 1700 and the beginning of 1800.

1st Room - Early Italians and Byzantines.

2nd Room - Giotto and followers.

3rd Room - Beato Angelico - Here are exposed some very small tableaux by this famous 15th century painter, among which are two episodes of the life of St. Nicholas of Bari, of an almost miniature nature, and the celebrated, most delicate Virgin and Child, among Sts. Domenic, Catherine and Angels, also this one is of tiny dimensions.

4th Room - Melozzo da Forlì - This powerful 15th century painter knew how to give deep expression to his works of the "humanistic" character of his times, which was abstracted from the vivid and working admiration for classic antiquity.

5th Room - Minor painters of the 15th century.

6th Room - 15th century polyptychos.

7th Room - 15th century Umbrian School - The room constitutes an interesting vestibule to the following room, entirely dedicated to Raphael: it presents, in fact, works of Umbrian artists, belonging to the same region as the great painter, some of whom are particularly tied to him. Here in fact is a painting by Perugino, Raphael's master: the **Virgin and Child and four Saints**, and a picture by Giovanni Santi, Raphael's father, representing St. Jerome.

8th Room - Raphael - The room houses three of the most famous paintings and ten tapestries of the great master from Urbino. On the large wall in front of the entrance we can admire the three great paintings. On the right is the **Coronation of the Virgin**, an early work of the artist, painted in 1503. On the left is the **Foligno Madonna**, which Raphael executed in Rome in 1512, at the time of the greatest splendour of his art. The composition has become

Raphael. The Transfiguration.

free and personal; a rich colour animates the scene, characterised by a perfect balance between Heaven and earth. At the centre, finally, is exposed the celebrated **Transfiguration**, which Raphael left unfinished at his sudden death which struck him down in 1520, at the age of only thirty-seven. The painting was exposed in the Sistine Chapel, before the deeply moved Romans, during the artist's funeral.

9th Room - Leonardo da Vinci - The visitor is impressed by **St. Jerome** by Leonardo da Vinci, left unfortunately unfinished, like many, too many works of that genial artist, writer and scientist of the Renaissance, whose uneasy and multiform genius did not allow him to dedicate himself intensely to any activity. While on the landscape background some traces of colour are unfolded, the expressive figure of the Saint and the mighty lion nestling at his feet are only drawn on the canvas, prepared with an ochre-coloured ground. In front of this is a

precious painting by another great artist who lived between the 15th and 16th centuries: the **Burial of Christ** by the Venetian Giovanni Bellini or "Giambellino".

10th Room - Titian, Veronese and various 16th century artists - The room is dominated by the immense **Madonna de' Frari**, a typical work of the most representative painter of Venice, Titian.

11th Room - Muziano and Barocci - Among the others as Ludovico Caracci, Giorgio Vasari, Cavalier d'Arpino, Girolamo Muziano and Federico Barocci stand out, both notable representatives of the Roman artistic circle.

12th Room - Baroque painters - This Room, of an octagonal shape, presents paintings of considerable dimensions of the most representative figures of the 17th century. The visitor is struck above all by the **Deposition of Christ from the Cross** by Caravaggio. Despite the lofty quality of the Caravaggio canvas, we cannot exempt ourselves from dwelling on other very estimable works exposed

Raphael. The Madonna of Foligno.

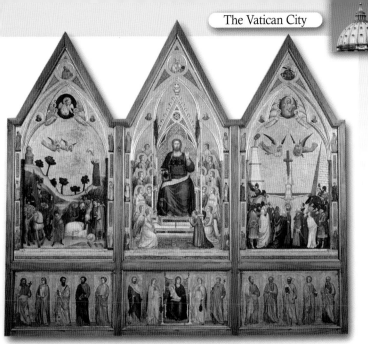

Giotto. Polittico Stefaneschi. *Tempera on wood (1315).*

in the same room: the **Crucifixion of St. Peter**, placed to the right of the Caravaggio painting, the work of Guido Reni and the **Communion of St. Jerome** by Domenichino, with a theatrically scenographic composition.

13th Room - Painters of the 17th and 18th centuries.

14th Room - Painters of various nationalities of the 17th and 18th centuries. Very popular, finally, is the Virgin and Child by Sassoferrato, a painter clever above all in design.

15th Room - Portraits from the 16th to the 19th centuries.

16th, 17th, 18th Rooms - Painters of the 19th and 20th centuries, among them we remember paintings and sculptures work of modern artists as Rodin, Fazzini, Morandi, Carrà, Greco, Manzù and Villon.

Another modern building, completed in 1970 by the architects Tullio and Vincenzo Passarelli at the request of Pope John XXIII, houses the most interesting collections from the Lateran Museums. There are three sections: the **Gregorian Profane Museum** with exhibits from archaeological excavations from the former Pontifical State, divided in two sections (I: Roman copies and imitations of Greek originals, II: Roman sculpture from the 1st century B.C. to the 2nd century A.D.); **Pio Christian Museum**, founded by Pope Pius IX in 1854, containing material which comes mostly from the catacombs and the ancient Christian basilicas; the **Ethnological Missionary Museum**, housing numerous sacred objects from all over the world. The rest of the Vatican City is a small, extraordinary world which cannot be described here, due to lack of space. However, it must be mentioned that the most important architectural contribution of the twentieth century is the great **Pontifical Audience Hall**, designed by Pier Luigi Nervi (1971), which is entered through the "Arco delle Campane" for the Pope's weekly audiences and other special events.

Useful Information

An asterisk is listed after the coordinates (ex.: via del Fiume B4*) when the streets are not shown on the map.

Anagnina Metro Station of line A. The price is € 1.20. *Line Termini Station - Ciampino Airport* - ticket € 3.90.

Arrivals and Departures by train

The principle train station in Rome is Termini Station (Piazza dei Cinquecento). Inside there is also a large shopping centre. Situated in a central position, numerous bus lines and subway lines depart from this station to all parts of the city. It

CITY NEWS

In Rome, the capital of Italy, there are nearly three million people. With a surface area of 129.000 hectares (around 1300 square Km), it is equal to nine average Italian cities and is the largest in Europe. The historic centre, including the area inside the Aurelian Walls and the first Municipality, extends as far as a medium-sized Italian city.

is also possible to arrive and depart from Tiburtina or Ostiense station, especially if you are travelling at night.

How to arrive and depart by car

One of the chronic problems in Rome is certainly the intense traffic and the difficulties in finding parking. It is not advisable to use a car for touring the city, as the historical centre and certain areas of interest are closed to private vehicles. It is preferable to leave the car well parked in roadside parking places or in a long term parking garage – such as Villa Borghese – and move around the city by using public transportation, walking or renting a scooter. Most of the parking in the city does require payment (up until 11:00 pm), and this is indicated by the blue lines surrounding the spaces, the fee is € 1.00 per hour.

TRANSPORT

Arrivals and Departures by plane

www.adr.it - There are two international airports in Rome: **Leonardo Da Vinci in Fiumicino** (tel. 06.65951) and **G.B. Pastine in Ciampino** (tel. 06.794941).

Arriving and Departing at "Leonardo da Vinci" airport in Fiumicino

The intercontinental Leonardo Da Vinci airport is connected to the centre of Rome by train, the "Leonardo Express" and the Metropolitan Train FM1, or by taxi, bus and even a highway that arrives in the EUR district of the city; it is also connected to the Grande Raccordo Anulare (the ring road highway that circles the perimeter of Rome).

Public City Transports

www.atac.roma.it - www.metroroma.it
In the city there are buses, subways, trams and electric busses. The ticket (B.I.T.) is valid for 75 minutes and costs €1.00 and allows for using all of the buses, but it only allows for one single trip in the underground subway or urban subway trains.

Arriving and Departing at "G. B. Pastine" airport in Ciampino by bus

Every 30 minutes from (from 6:30am to 11:00pm)/to (from 6:15am to 10:30pm)

The tickets range from (€ 4.00 for a full day up to € 16.00 for a week) and can be bought at newsstands, tobacconist shops, kiosks displaying the Atac/Cotral logo and the major train stations. There are two metro lines: A (the red line) and B (the blue line). These two lines intersect at Termini station. Subway service begins at 5:30 am and ends at 11:30 pm on Saturdays until 12:30 am. Busses and trams function from 5:30 am until midnight and it is not possible to buy tickets on board. From midnight until 5 am there are some night busses available (indicated by the letter N) and it is possible to buy a ticket on board.

TAXI
Radiotaxi - tel. 068822 - 066645 - 064157 - 063570 - 064994
For a taxi from the historic centre (including the entire area inside the Aurelian Walls) to the two main Rome airports, a fixed rate is applied: 35 Euros to Ciampino Airport and 45 Euros to Fiumicino Airport. For other destinations the price is calculated by the taxi meter. Supplemental fees: bag

€ 1.00 - nights (from 10 pm to 7 am) € 3.50, Sundays and holidays € 1.00.

TOURIST BUSES
Ciao Roma Open Bus, tel. 0647886623. Open air double-decked busses in English style for viewing the city from above with the stop&go formula. Ticket price € 19.00 everyday, afternoon price (after 1:30 pm) € 15.00. One non-stop 2 hour course is € 12.00.

River Boats of Rome, tel. 066789361. www.battellidiroma.it

BICYCLE RENTAL
For visiting the historic centre, bicycle rental is advisable, due to the extraordinary size of the historic area and the city's mild climate. The largest bike rental areas are Largo dei Lombardi (B4*), Piazza del Popolo (B4) and Villa Borghese (Pincio) (A4). Prices range from 3 Euros per hour to 10 Euros per day.

SCOOTER RENTAL
Hundreds of thousands of Romans choose scooters for their daily driving needs. This can also provide a great way for tourists to get around the city and to save time. It is easy to find parking, it is possible to enter into the limited traffic areas and traffic jams are not a risk, in many cases compensating the risks connected with driving in the city's unruly traffic.
It is necessary to have a license or for minors, a scooter license to rent a 50 cc scooter. It is obligatory to use a helmet. The daily fee starts at around 30 Euros.

Eco Move Rent, Via Varese 48/50 (BC7) - tel. 06.44704518
Roma Rent, Vicolo de' Bovari, 7a (C4*) - tel. 06.6896555
Scooter for Rent, Via della Purificazione 64 (BC*)- tel. 06.4885485

TOURIST INFORMATION

APT, Visitor Center, via Parigi, 5 (B6). Tel. 0648899212. Hours: Mon.-Sat. 9am-7pm. www.romaturismo.it
The Vatican City, tel. 0669881662. www.vatican.va.
Rome Municipality - call center tel. 060606. www.comune.roma.it

Useful Information

An asterisk is listed after the coordinates (ex.: via del Fiume B4*) when the streets are not shown on the map.

Archeologia Card, is valid for seven days and provides entrance to the following sites: Coliseum, Palatine, Caracalla Baths, Villa dei Quintilli, Tomb of Cecilia Metella, Diocletian's Baths, Crypta Balbi, Palazzo Altemps and Palazzo Massimo. € 23.00. **Roma Pass**, is valid for three days: € 25.00. Roma Pass gives free admission to the first two museums and/or archaeological sites, full access to the public transport system, reduced tickets and discounts for the other museums, sites and events. Tel. 0682059127. www.romapass.it **Museums and archaeological sites, informations and reservations. 060608** is a telephone number for requesting information in five different languages on tourism, shows and cultural events in Rome or for buying tickets to theatre events, concerts and museums as well as providing some cinema information: For all this plus hotel, restaurant and a great deal of other information, visit the website www.060608.it.

MONUMENTS

Ara Pacis, Piazza Augusto Imperatore (B4). Tel. 0682059127. Ticket € 7.50. Hours: 9am-7pm. Closed on Mondays. www.arapacis.it

Baths of Caracalla, Viale d. Terme di Caracalla, 52 (EF6). Tel. 0639967700. Ticket € 6.00. Hours: from 9am to one hour before sunset. Monday 9am-2pm.

Castel Sant'Angelo National Museum, Lungotevere Castello, 50 (C3). Tel. 066819111. Ticket € 5.00. Hours: 9am-7:30pm. Closed on Mondays. www.castelsantangelo.com

Colosseum, Piazza del Colosseo (D6). Tel. 0639967700. Ticket € 12.00. Ticket is also valid for the Palatino and Roman Forum. Hours: from 9am to one hour before sunset.

Palatino, Piazza Santa Maria Nova, 53 (D5*) / Via di San Gregorio, 30. Tel. 0639967700.

Ticket € 12.00. Ticket is also valid for the Colosseum and Roman Forum. Hours: from 9am to one hour before sunset:

Pantheon, Piazza della Rotonda (C4*). Tel. 0668300230. Free entrance. Hours: 8:30am-7:30pm. Sun. 9am-6pm.

Roman Forum, Largo Romolo e Remo, 2 (E5*). Tel. 0639967700. Ticket € 12.00. Ticket is also valid for the Colosseum and 9am to one hour before sunset.

Trajan's Market - Museum of the Imperial Fora, Via IV Novembre, 94 (C5). Tel. 060608. Ticket € 8.50. Hours: 9am-7pm. Closed on Mondays. www.mercatiditraiano.it

Vittoriano, Piazza Venezia (D5). Tel. 066991718. Free entrance. Hours: 9:30am-4:30pm.

MUSEUMS AND GALLERIES

Ancient Art National Gallery (Palazzo Barberini), Via Quattro Fontane, 13 (C5-6). Tel. 064824184. Ticket € 5.00. Hours: 8:30am-7:30pm. Closed on Mondays. www.galleriaborghese.it

Borghese Museum and Gallery, Villa Borghese. Piazzale Scipione Borghese, 5 (A6*). Tel. 0632810. Ticket € 6.50; (reservation, € 2.00). Tel. 0632810.). Hours: 9am-7pm. Closed on Mondays. www.galleriaborghese.it

Capitolini Museums, Piazza del Campidoglio, 1 (D5). Tel. 060608. Ticket € 8.50. Hours: 9am-8pm. Closed on Mondays. www.museicapitolini.org

Etruscan National Museum, P.le di Villa Giulia, 9 (A4*). Tel. 063226571. Ticket € 4,00. Hours: 8:30am-7:30pm. Closed on Mondays. http://villagiulia.beniculturali.it

MACRO - Rome's Museum of Contemporary Art, Via Reggio Emilia, 54 (B7). Tel. 060608. Ticket € 11.00. Hours: 11am-10pm. Closed on Mondays. www.macro.roma.museum

MAXXI - National Museum 21th century Arts, Via Guido Reni, 4a. Tel. 0639967350. Ticket € 11.00. Hours: tue/sun 11am-7pm; thu 11am-10pm. Closed on Mondays. www.fondazionemaxxi.it

Modern Art National Gallery GNAM, Viale delle Belle Arti, 131 (A5*). Tel. 0632298221. Ticket € 12.00. Hours: 8:30am-7:30pm. Closed on Mondays. www.gnam.beniculturali.it
Roman Civilization Museum, Piazza G. Agnelli, 10 (Eur). Tel. 060608. Ticket € 7.50. Hours: 9am-2pm. Closed on Mondays. www.museociviltaromana.it
Roman National Museum, Tel. 0639967700. Closed on Mondays. Ticket € 7.00:
  Palazzo Altemps, Piazza Sant'Apollinare, 46 (C4*). Hours: 9am-7:45pm.
  Palazzo Massimo alle Terme, Largo Villa Peretti, 1 (C6-7*). Hours: 9am-7:45pm.
  Terme di Diocleziano, Viale Enrico De Nicola, 78 (C7). Hours: 9am-7:45pm.
Vatican Museums, Viale Vaticano (BC1). Tel. 06.69884947. Ticket € 15.00. Hours: 8:30am-4pm. Closed on Sundays. Open the las Sunday of each month (free entrance). Visits to Vatican Gardens call Tel. 0669884466. www.vatican.va

CHURCHES AND BASILICAS
Holy Cross in Jerusalem, Piazza S. Croce in G., 12 (E8). Tel. 067014769
St. Agnes outside the Walls, Via Nomentana, 349. Tel. 068610840
St. Agnes in Agone, Piazza Navona (C4). Tel. 0668192134
St. Cecilia in Trastevere, Piazza Santa Cecilia, 22 (E4). Tel. 065899289
St. Clement, Piazza San Clemente (D6*). Tel. 0670451018
St. John Lateran, Piazza San Giovanni in Laterano (E7). Tel. 0669886464
St. Lawrence outside the Walls, Piazzale del Verano, 3 (C9). Tel. 06491511
St. Mary in Aracoeli, Piazza del Campidoglio, 4 (D5). Tel. 066798155
St. Mary in Cosmedin, Piazza Bocca della Verità (E4). Tel. 066781419.
St. Mary in Trastevere, Piazza Santa Maria in T. (D3). Tel. 065814802
St. Mary Major, Piazza Santa Maria Maggiore (C7). Tel. 064881094
St. Mary of the Angels, Piazza della Repubblica (C6). Tel. 064880812
St. Paul outside the Walls, Piazzale San Paolo. Tel. 065410341
St. Peter in the Vatican, Piazza San Pietro (C2). Tel. 0669883462
St. Peter in Vincoli, Piazza San Pietro in Vincoli, 4a (D6*). Tel. 064882865.

CATACOMBS
Domitilla, Via delle Sette Chiese, 282. Tel. 065110342. Hours: 9am-12pm/2pm-5pm. Ticket € 8.00. Closed on Tuesdays.
San Callisto, Via Appia Antica, 110. Tel. 065136725. Hours: 9am-12pm 2pm-5pm. Ticket € 8.00. Closed on Wednesdays.
San Sebastiano, Via Appia Antica, 136. Tel. 067887035. Hours: 9am-12pm 2pm-5pm. Ticket € 8.00. Closed on Sundays.

ENJOY ROME

To truly taste the flavour of the city requires living like the Romans - a big "yes" to culture, art and entertainment, but also to relaxing in the sun and enjoying fine food. Every Roman's day begins with the coffee ritual, which is always espresso coffee – or cappuccino – that is drunk while standing at the bar and eating a cornetto (croissant). This traditional breakfast sweet can be filled with cream or jam. Lunch generally includes a light pizza snack, a salad or a sandwich (tramezzini triangle-shaped sandwiches can be found in most bars), but there are also Romans who prefer to sit down at a full service restaurant to enjoy a tasty dish of pasta. To placate unexpected munchies during the day, we suggest a short break and pizza sold by the slice (pizza a taglio) or ice cream (gelato) during the summers. Around 7 pm Romans enjoy an aperitif with a glass of wine, a cocktail and a snack.

For dinner, many Romans enjoy the rite of pizza, individual-sized pizzas, in one of the many versions available – margherita, napoletana, or capricciosa eaten in fun and laid back environments. The city is teeming with life after dinner as well, thanks to a mild climate and the sunny, friendly disposition of its inhabitants. A large part of Roman life takes place outside, and even late at night the people stroll throughout the piazzas and streets in the centre, stopping in at café's, cocktail bars, or entertaining themselves at discos, live concerts and at the movies.

Among the most happening zones for nightlife we suggest the areas surrounding Piazza Navona and the Pantheon (C4), Campo de' Fiori (CD4) and Trastevere; for those wanting to go outside the historic centre, the Via Libetta area in the Ostiense neighbourhood and via di Monte Testaccio (F4) are recommended. From June until September the city is animated with numerous Estate Romana (Roman Summer) initiatives promoted by the City of Rome including concerts, events and presentations of classical music, jazz and movies.

EATING IN ROME
Roman cuisine follows the Mediterranean diet and is made up of simple dishes such as pasta and a few of the most famous are – cacio e pepe, all'amatriciana, alla gricia or pomodoro. Meat dishes include – lamb, beef or chicken that has been baked or grilled – seafood dishes and an infinite choice of cooked or raw seasonal vegetables (broccoli rabe, escarole and artichokes) that are typically eaten as side dishes together with second course meat dishes. The world famous wines of the

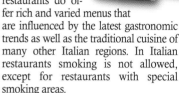

Piedmont Region and Tuscany have frequently overshadowed the wines from Lazio, which over the last years have had impressive quality levels. All said, most restaurants do offer rich and varied menus that are influenced by the latest gastronomic trends as well as the traditional cuisine of many other Italian regions. In Italian restaurants smoking is not allowed, except for restaurants with special smoking areas.

SHOPPING

Rome offers its visitors not only art and dining but also a multitude of possibilities for high quality shopping, especially for fashion items, without necessarily having to spend a fortune. Many streets are filled with stores, but for exploring the city's fashion district we suggest the roads that surround the Spanish Steps (Via del Babuino, Via Condotti, Via della Croce, and Via Borgognona) (B4-5) where the most renowned names in fashion can be found. Stores are open from 9:00am until 1:00pm and from 3:30pm to 7:30pm (on summer until 8pm). Many stores are closed all day Sunday and Monday mornings.

HOSPITALITY

www.romaturismo.it
www.rome-hotels.it
www.bedandbreakfastroma.com
www.hostelbookers.com/hostels/italy/rome

EMERGENCY TELEPHONE NUMBERS

Ambulance	.065510
Carabinieri	112
Rome Municipality	.060606
Medical services	.06570600
Police - Emergency	.113
Traffic & Highway Police	.0664686
First Aid	.118
Fire Brigade	.115
Municipal Police	.0667691

SUBWAY AND URBAN RAIL MAP

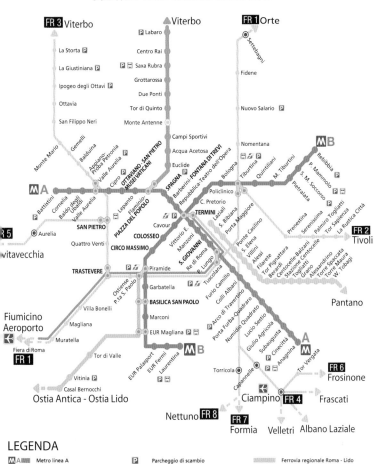

LEGENDA

Ⓜ A	Metro linea A	Ⓟ Parcheggio di scambio
Ⓜ B	Metro linea B	Capolinea bus extraurbani
	Ferrovia regionale Roma - Viterbo	◉ Limite di validità della tariffa urbana Metrebus Roma
	Ferrovia regionale Roma - Pantano	◉ Collegamento bus da FS Ciampino a Aeroporto Ciampino

Ferrovia regionale Roma - Lido	
Ferrovie regionali	
Stazione di scambio (metro-ferrovia)	

THE ETERNAL CITY

© LOZZI ROMA s.a.s.

ISBN 978-88-86843-18-8

Periodico annuale - Anno XVI - Edizione 2012
Registrazione Tribunale di Roma n. 625/96
Direttore responsabile Franco Rossi Marcelli

Publisher: LOZZI ROMA S.a.s.
Via Filippo Nicolai, 91 - 00136 Roma
Tel. (+39) 06 35497051 / 06 97841668
Fax 06 35497074
e-mail: info@lozziroma.com
web: www.gruppolozzi.it

Photographies:
Archivio fotografico Fabbrica di San Pietro
Archivio fotografico Musei e Gallerie Pontificie
Archivio fotografico Osservatore Romano
Editrice Millenium s.r.l.
Lozzi Roma s.a.s.
Photo SCALA, Firenze

Graphic Reconstructions of Ancient Rome:
Archeolibri srl. Made by My Max.

Printed by: C.S.C. Grafica srl - Roma
Made in Italy

The blue lines trace the itineraries described in the guide-book